As one of the world's longest established and best-known travel brands, Thomas Cook are the experts in travel.

For more than 135 years our guidebooks have unlocked the secrets of destinations around the world, sharing with travellers a wealth of experience and a passion for travel.

Rely on Thomas Cook as your travelling companion on your next trip and benefit from our unique heritage.

Thomas Cook **traveller** guides

CYPRUS
Robert Bulmer

Written by Robert Bulmer, updated by Carole French
Original photography by Malcolm Birkitt

Published by Thomas Cook Publishing
A division of Thomas Cook Tour Operations Limited
Company registration no. 3772199 England
The Thomas Cook Business Park, Unit 9, Coningsby Road,
Peterborough PE3 8SB, United Kingdom
Email: books@thomascook.com, Tel: +44 (0) 1733 416477
www.thomascookpublishing.com

Produced by Cambridge Publishing Management Limited
Burr Elm Court, Main Street, Caldecote CB23 7NU
www.cambridgepm.co.uk

ISBN: 978-1-84848-391-0

© 2002, 2005, 2007, 2009 Thomas Cook Publishing
This fifth edition © 2011
Text © Thomas Cook Publishing
Maps © Thomas Cook Publishing/PCGraphics (UK) Limited

Series Editor: Karen Beaulah
Production/DTP: Steven Collins

Printed and bound in Spain by GraphyCems

Cover photography © Photononstop/SuperStock

Contents

Introduction

When powerful geological forces formed the island of Cyprus in the warm waters of the Mediterranean they created two very different mountain ranges (see pp6–7) separated by a remarkable flat plain and a splendid coastline of bays, inlets and beaches. Nature then took the opportunity offered to exploit these features to the fullest and this is most wonderfully demonstrated in the springtime, when the whole island is transformed by wild flowers into a blaze of colour.

Today, Cyprus is in the hands of other powerful forces. Holiday towns have blossomed in areas that were once covered by nothing but bushes and sand dunes. Europeans in their millions, and especially the British, are abandoning the grey winter skies of home to settle in Cyprus for much of the year. Villas and apartments are everywhere, nowhere more so than in the country north of Pafos, where the hillsides, white with dwellings, rise into the distance. Even so, it is still possible to find a corner of Cyprus hardly changed, most likely in a remote village, or perhaps in the northern part of Lefkosia (Nicosia). Here the shops never seem to change, with their miscellany of goods spilling into the street, just as they have for many years.

An important change for holidaymakers is the steady increase in costs. Progress and membership of the European Union have brought prices ever closer to those of Western Europe. The hospitality of the Cypriot is no longer outrageously generous, at least not in the tourist centres. Nevertheless, it is still impossible to get through the holiday without being offered a free drink or some delicious fruit; and in the villages the irrepressible desire to please is undiminished.

Highways now connect the towns of Lefkosia (Nicosia), Larnaka, Lemesos (Limassol) and Pafos. This is good news for visitors in a hurry for it will cut the journey time by half. Unfortunately, they will miss all the villages en route, but a detour of a few kilometres brings one to an older Cyprus where life goes on much as it always did.

'History in this island is almost too profuse. It gives me a sort of mental indigestion.'
ROBERT BYRON
The Road to Oxiana, 1937
'Realising that they will never be a world power, the Cypriots have decided for being a world nuisance.'
GEORGE MIKES
The Times, 1980

Cyprus is an island with something for everybody. Young (and not so young) sun-worshippers and clubbers pour into Lemesos, Agia Napa and Protaras from all over Europe. They undoubtedly have the time of their lives, their evenings can be long, and many go straight from the nightspots to the beaches, saving breakfast for midday. Other visitors find the quiet beaches of Chrysochou Bay, the Troodos Mountains and the laid-back feel of northern Cyprus to their liking. Indeed, while the Greek-speaking Cypriots are struggling to conserve what remains of their coastline, the Turkish-speaking Cypriots have a relatively unspoilt territory.

Cyprus lies at a crossroads between East and West. Settled first by peoples from Asia Minor and Anatolia (modern Turkey), then Mycenae (Greece), over the centuries it has been subjected to a multitude of different cultures.

PLACE NAMES

Place names in Cyprus can be confusing, with colonial era, modern Greek and Turkish names all in use. Nicosia is known to its Greek-Cypriot population as Lefkosia and to its Turkish-Cypriot population as Lefkoşa; Limassol is now Lemesos; Paphos is now Pafos; Larnaca is now Larnaka; and in the north Famagusta is Gazimağusa, while Kyrenia is now known as Girne.

The Greek- and Turkish-Cypriot communities no longer live side by side – they are separated by a line that runs from coast to coast. Today, the divide can be crossed on a daily basis and, following the 2008 election of leftist Greek-Cypriot President Dimitris Christofias, it seems likely the artificial border may be removed and the country unified once again.

Hospitality and friendliness are a feature of the north and the south. For the visitor, this means a warm welcome wherever they go. For most travellers a trip to Cyprus often turns out to be the holiday of a lifetime.

Introduction

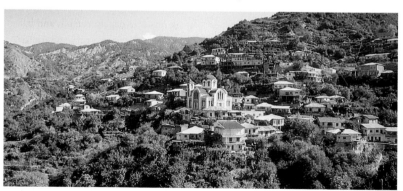

The village of Moutoullas, set in the rock of the Troodos Mountains

The land

Cyprus is the third-largest island in the Mediterranean after Sardinia and Sicily, but still only 240km (149 miles) long and 100km (62 miles) wide. A large central plain has mountains to the north – Beşparmak (Pentadaktylos) and Karpaz Yarımadası (Karpasia) – and the south – Troodos – and there is a varied coastline. Its situation at the far eastern end of the Mediterranean, close to the Middle East but detached from it, is vital to understanding the nature and history of Cyprus.

By virtue of its position the island has long been of great strategic importance, and any power with an interest in the Middle East has also had an interest in Cyprus.

The island's culture, language and people are firstly Cypriot, with Greek and Turkish influences evident in their cultures, languages and cuisines. The island is physically closer to the Muslim world. Turkey is only 69km (43 miles) away, Syria 95km (59 miles) distant, while Athens lies at a distance of 800km (497 miles).

Geology

The geological origins of Cyprus are still open to debate, but most current theories propose the view that the island was formed by some kind of underwater explosion. This is definitely true of the Troodos Mountains, which are made of igneous rock thrust up by continental plates in prehistory.

The initial geological instability meant that Cyprus suffered from frequent earthquakes during its early history. Many of the prehistoric sites on the south coast were badly damaged by such quakes. The last significant one was on 9 October 1996 and measured 6.5 in magnitude.

Mountains

The island is dominated by two mountain ranges: the Troodos and the Beşparmak. The former range is the higher, with Mount Olympos rising to 1,952m (6,404ft). This altitude ensures snow cover through much of the winter. The higher slopes of the range are covered in trees, but there are also vineyards.

The height of the mountains means that even in summer the temperature is much lower than on the plain below. While the summer sees little rainfall, the winter rains and the melting snow are a vital resource.

The Troodos are also the source of many of Cyprus's minerals. Copper has been mined here since 3000 BC and may be the source of the island's name, Kypros, in Greek.

The mountains descend gently towards Lemesos and the southern coast. In total contrast, the northern slopes in the Polis area come down to the sea in spectacularly steep fashion.

The mountains of the Beşparmak range are made of sedimentary rocks and are about half as high as the Troodos, but can be more impressive due to their craggy outline. Most notable is Mount Beşparmak (Pentadaktylos in Greek), which means 'five fingers', after its resemblance to five stumpy digits.

Historically, there was extensive deforestation of all the mountains, originally to provide wood to build the fleets of distant monarchs, including Alexander the Great, but in later years because of overgrazing. The forestry department has worked hard to reverse this, and there are several extensive forests in the west of the Troodos.

The coast and the plains

The coastline is extremely varied, ranging from inaccessible rocky coves to extensive sandy beaches. There are two natural harbours, at Lemesos and Gazimağusa (Famagusta).

In between the two mountain ranges is the Mesaoria Plain on which the island's capital Lefkosia can be found. It is a relatively fertile area, although at the end of summer it resembles a dust bowl. The main agricultural activity takes place in spring; after that, the lack of water takes its toll and rivers dry up.

In the far east is the narrow jutting segment of land known as the Karpaz in Turkish. This beautiful remote area has experienced little development and is a protected nature reserve with some of the country's best beaches.

The economy

Despite the lack of water – it rarely rains between April and October – one of the mainstays of the Cypriot economy is agriculture. In the east, windmills were once employed to pump irrigation water on to the potato crops. Most of these are now redundant due to the introduction of desalination plants. Around Lemesos and in the north near Güzelyurt (Morfou) are extensive citrus groves, and vineyards virtually everywhere.

Tourism is now the main source of income for the island. There are nearly three million visitors each year, and nearly every Cypriot has some interest in the industry, fuelling the debate as to how much more development of this industry the island can sustain.

Nissi Beach is a tourist favourite

The land

N

Acheiropoietos
Monastery
Beylerb
(Bellap.
Lambusa
(Lampousa)
Karaku
(Karakoum
Koruçam Burnu
(Akrotirio Kormakitis)
Güzelyali
(Vavylas)
Girne
(Kyrenia)
Kayalar (Orga)
Lapta
(Lapithos)
Agios
Ilarion
Bella
Paleokastro
Camlibel
(Myrtou)
Güzelyurt Körfezi
(Kolpos Morfou)
Karavas
Loutra Afroditis
(Baths of Aphrodite)
Erenköy
(Kokkina)
Kato
Pyrgos
Güzelyurt
(Morfou)
Agios Mamas
LEFKOSIA/LEFKOSA
(NICOSIA)
Fontana
Amorosa
Akra
Pomou
Vuni
(Vouni)
Soloi
Lefke
(Lefka)
Peristerona
A9
Akrotirio
Arnaoutis
Kolpos
Chrysochou
Agios Ioannis
Lampadistis
B9
Akaki
Marion
Kalopanagiotis
Agios Nikolaos
tis Stegis
Nikitari
Agios
Irakleidios
Akamas
Stavros tis Psokas
Asinou
Stavros tou
Klirou
Politiko
Tamass
Kolpos Lara
Latchi
Polis
Koilada tou Kedron
Throni Kykkos
Galata
Agiasmati
Turtle
Hatchery
Drouseia
(Cedar Valley)
Kakopetria
Panagia
tou Araka
Fikardou
Skoulli
Pano
Pedoulas
Prodromos
Akrotirio
Drepanon
Pegeia
B7
Panagia
Panagia
Moutoullas
Troodos
1952m
Machaira
Chrysorrogiatissa
Gefyra Kelephou
Troodos
Kyperounta
Agios
Georgios
Agiou
Neofytou
Polemi
(Kelephos Bridge)
Trooditissa
Papoutsa
Maa-Palaeokastro
Galataria
Pano Platres
1562m
Ora
Lefka
Ormos
Korallion
(Coral Bay)
Grivas
Museum
Empa
Agia Moni
Omodos
Arakapas
Skarinot
Gefyra Roudia
(Roudhias Bridge)
Choirokoitia
(Khirokitia)
Chlorakas
Geroskipou
(Yeroskipos)
Camel
Trail
Arsos
Pachna
B8
Ieron Appollonos
(Yermasoyia)
Germasogeia
(Yermasoyia)
Moni
Zy
Pafos (Paphos)
Dora
Palaepaphos
Avdimou
(Evdhimou)
(Sanctuary of
Apollo Hylates)
A1
Kato Pafos
Pafos
Int.
Agia
Timi
A6
Amathous
Govern
Beach
Leondios
Kouklia
Episkopi
Kolossi
Fasouri
Lemesos (Limasso
Petra tou Romiou
Pissouri
Kourion
Salt Lake
Kolpos Akrotirion
Akrotirio
Aspro
Kolpos
Episkopi
Lady's Mile Beach
Akrotirion (Akrotiri)
Agiou Nikolaou ton Gaton
Akrotirio
Zevgari
Akrotirio
Gata

History

Stone Age 7000–2500 BC	The first settlers come to Cyprus from Asia Minor (modern-day Turkey).
Bronze Age 2500–1050 BC	Immigration from Anatolia (modern Turkey) and later from Mycenae (modern Greece). There is rapid development of bronze implements, jewellery and ceramics. Trade takes place with other eastern Mediterranean peoples.
Iron Age 1050–325 BC	Cultural innovation and the building of new cities. Metallurgy flourishes and pottery develops.
10th century BC	Phoenicians arrive and subjugate the island.
8th century BC	Assyrian rule, but Cyprus's kings exercise local authority.
7th–6th centuries BC	Assyrian Empire collapses with the Egyptians assuming control of the island in 570 BC.
545 BC	Cyprus submits to Persian domination.
325 BC	Start of Hellenistic period with Alexander the Great's victory at Tyre. Shortly after, the Ptolemies of Egypt capture Cyprus.
58 BC	Roman annexation. Their legacy of public building is seen today with the Sanctuary of Apollo Hylates at Kourion, the Temple of Zeus at Salamis, and Nea Pafos and Soloi.
AD 330	Division of the Roman Empire (Byzantine period); Cyprus is ruled from Constantinople. The Church of Cyprus becomes fully established.
647	Arab attacks over the next 300 years weaken Byzantine control.
750	The Byzantines reassert their authority; 100 years later the second golden age of Byzantium commences, lasting another 300 years.
1191	Richard the Lionheart, on his Crusade to the Holy Lands, makes landfall near Lemesos (*see p65*). Richard sells Cyprus to the Knights Templar in 1192, but takes the island back before

passing the island to crusading Frankish knight Guy de Lusignan.

1192–1489 The Lusignans rule for nearly 300 years. In 1489, the Venetians, asked to help repel a Genoese invasion, annex the island for themselves.

1489–1571 Venetian rule – a period noted for persecution of the Cypriot-Greek Church. The Venetians construct massive defences. Famagusta and Lefkosia (Nicosia) are encircled by walls and bastions, which survive today. However, the Ottoman Turks storm Lefkosia in 1570 and Famagusta surrenders in 1571.

1571–1878 Ottoman rule. The island is settled by the Turkish Ottomans, resulting in the creation of two communities living side by side. Surprisingly, the Cypriot-Greek Orthodox Church rises again in this period and the archbishop acquires power.

1878 The Ottoman Empire cedes the island to Great Britain for administrative and defence purposes, though it remains under the authority of the sultan. As a British colony Cyprus prospers.

1914 Turkey enters World War I on Germany's side. Cyprus is formally annexed to Great Britain.

1923 Turkey renounces claims to the island. Greek Cypriots demand Union with Greece (Enosis).

1955–9 The National Organisation of Cypriot Combatants (EOKA) pursues a terror campaign against Turkish Cypriots. Zurich and London Agreement signed in which Britain, Greece and Turkey guarantee the new republic's independence.

1960–64 Archbishop Makarios III becomes president. Hostilities between the communities flare up in 1963. Turkish Cypriots retreat into enclaves in the north, Greek Cypriots to the south. UN peacekeeping forces sent in to the area in 1964.

1967 EOKA recommences its campaign for Enosis.

1974	EOKA, supported by the Greek military junta, carries out a coup against Makarios. Five days later, Turkish forces invade northern Cyprus to protect Turkish Cypriots. Talks are unsuccessful.
1983	Turkish Cypriots declare the independence of northern Cyprus.
1992	Talks between the leaders of the two communities take place. The UN reduces the area held by Turkish Cypriots. Talks collapse.
2003	Border restrictions lifted for Greek and Turkish Cypriots. There are renewed hopes of a solution.
2004	UN (Annan Plan) referendum held for reunification of island – Turkish Cypriots vote for, Greek Cypriots against. Cyprus joins the European Union.
2008	The euro replaces the Cypriot pound in the south. Newly elected communist president Greek-Cypriot Dimitris Christofias makes unification top priority and meets Turkish leader Mehmet Ali Talat to resume talks. Ledra Street border crossing opened.
2010	Turkish-Cypriot leader Mehmet Ali Talat loses power to Derviş Eroğlu of the National Unity Party. Talks between Dimitris Christofias and Eroğlu continue. The Limnitis border checkpoint opens, the seventh crossing between the north and the south.
2011	A £25 million investment package in tourism is launched to create new attractions and open up new air routes.

Statue of President Makarios at the foot of Throni hill, in the Troodos region

Politics

When the newly appointed Greek-Cypriot President Dimitris Christofias announced that the reunification of north and south was his top priority in February 2008, and went on to meet the then Turkish leader Mehmet Ali Talat to discuss steps to make this happen, it was the first time leaders from both sides in the conflict had met in three decades.

Within weeks of the president's announcement, the barrier across the pedestrianised Ledra Street shopping area came down, enabling Greek Cypriots and Turkish Cypriots to cross freely. In October 2010 the Limnitas checkpoint near Kato Pyrgos in the northwest of the island opened. Reunification talks between President Christofias and Talat's successor, Derviş Eroğlu of the National Unity Party, continue.

Government and administration of Cyprus operate, in theory, as established in the 1960 constitution. The president is head of the executive and is elected every five years, as are members of the House of Representatives, from which the Council of Ministers is chosen. The parliament was to have 56 Greek-Cypriot members and 24 Turkish-Cypriot members. The executive was to be headed by a Greek-Cypriot president with a Turkish-Cypriot vice-president. Since 1964, following violent clashes, it has functioned with only the 56 Greek-Cypriot members.

The first presidential elections were won by Archbishop Makarios III, head of the Orthodox Church in Cyprus, who remained president until his death in 1977, apart from a short period of exile. In 2004, the UN Annan Plan referendum for unification was announced but, with key issues not addressed, it was rejected by the Greek Cypriots. A divided Cyprus joined the European Union the same year. In 2008, after three years of coalition government, the Greek Cypriots elected President Christofias.

In the north, a 'government' of 50 elected members was dominated for almost 30 years by Turkish-Cypriot leader Rauf Denktash, who stood down in 2004 after Turkish Cypriots overwhelmingly voted for unification (Denktash had opposed it), ushering in pro-unification leader Mehmet Ali Talat. Reunification talks stalled in 2009 after Talat's power weakened. In 2010, Derviş Eroğlu of the pro-independence National Unity Party succeeded Talat to become the Turkish-Cypriot leader.

The border

People not familiar with Cyprus's troubles can be unsettled at the first sight of United Nations soldiers. The soldiers taking their leave in the bars and cafés of the resorts may well give the impression of being on holiday themselves. However, they have been here on serious business, mainly to keep the peace between Greek and Turkish Cypriots. They first came in 1964 when the Turkish Cypriots retreated into enclaves in the north for safety and the Greek Cypriots retreated to the south. Since 1974 the division has run from Kato Pyrgos in the west to Gazimağusa in the east, passing through the centre of old Lefkosia. There are observation posts along the entire 200km (124-mile) border, where Greek Cypriots in the south face Turkish Cypriots in the north. The no man's land is held by the United Nations.

In Lefkosia's ancient walled town, Greek Cypriots and Turkish Cypriots

A border watchtower in Lefkosia

live in close proximity. In the aftermath of the 1974 fighting this was not a friendly confrontation, and every once in a while the night sky would explode into a firework display of tracer shells down the length of the line. Today, it is different; the advancing years have drawn the sting of anger and hatred. Turkish and Greek Cypriots freely cross from one side to the other to visit friends and family, and go sightseeing and shopping.

There are seven crossing points: one at the old Ledra Palace Hotel on the edge of the walled city of Lefkosia

THE GREEN LINE

The description 'Green Line' dates from the troubles of 1963–4 when Lefkosia was partitioned. A British intermediary drew a line in green ink on a map of the city. Now the term is used to describe the line in its island-wide entirety.

where sandbags and bullet-marked buildings create an air of disconcerting (and unnecessary) tension, Agios Dometios and Metehan in Lefkosia, Strovilia and Pergamos, and, opened in March 2008, a crossing at Ledra Street itself to make exploring the old town far easier than it has been in recent years.

The most recent crossing to open was the Limnitis checkpoint near Kato Pyrgos in 2010.

A Greek-Cypriot policeman will check passports and happily send you on your way, while on the Turkish-Cypriot side you will have to complete a form. If you're staying for a while, expect to have to open your bags for inspection on the Greek-Cypriot side. Taxis will also take you across and frequently do the trip to Ercan Airport. Cross it while you can – it may be gone soon.

Culture

Cyprus has not had any great impact on international culture. Furthermore, the few home-grown artists have tended to move abroad; not that this prevents the Cypriots claiming and celebrating them as their own. Zeno, the Stoic philosopher, was one such emigrant. He was born in Larnaka and is much celebrated there. But he left the island at an early age, and his Stoic philosophy of grinning and bearing the injustices of life was worked out in the intellectual hothouse of Athens.

Cyprus in mythology

Cyprus's culture is inextricably linked to its history and its place in early Greek mythology. Most impressively, the island is reputed to have been the birthplace of Aphrodite. She emerged from the waves at Petra tou Romiou, which is still a spectacular spot, an image providing inspiration for artists from around the world. The most famous painting to result is Botticelli's *Birth of Venus*, where she is depicted emerging from the waves upon a seashell.

Aphrodite kept a long-standing connection with the island and found several of her many lovers here, ranging from Akamas to Adonis. Her influence persists through the hundreds of cafés that have been named after her.

Further references appear in Homer's *The Odyssey*, which confirms Aphrodite's presence on the island: 'Pafos in Cyprus has her precinct and fragrant altar.' Visitors today can visit the Baths of Aphrodite near Polis, where legend has it the goddess bathed after a night of passion.

Cultural history

The Romans had little cultural impact except perhaps through their buildings; the best examples are the theatres at Salamis and Kourion.

The Lusignans, however, left a significant legacy of fine buildings in Gothic style and brought considerable Italian influence to the island.

Yet it was in the Byzantine period that Cyprus really flowered into a major cultural centre through icon painting in the churches across the island. These paintings, many of which are well preserved, are among the finest examples in the Mediterranean. Some of the best icon painters in Europe came to Cyprus to practise their art, such as Philip Goul, who decorated the churches of Stavros tou Agiasmati and Agios Mamas at Louvaras. The effort which went into painting literally hundreds of churches is extraordinary and has left a remarkable legacy.

The Turkish period seems to have seen a decline in cultural activity. However, there is a strong folk culture with a long tradition.

Folk art

There is a rich heritage of old folk ballads and poems which have been passed on, and which are now recited at festivals and village fairs. The folk music and dances have followed a similar pattern, though they tend only to be seen in displays for tourists.

There are other more tangible manifestations of folk art in pottery, jewellery and textiles. Fine examples of intricately sewn national costumes can be seen in folk museums across the island. Lefkara, a village in the hills east of Lemesos, is the home of lace making. The craft could date back to the Assyrian period since early lace has been found at Salamis. However, Cypriot lace did not gain international recognition until the 15th century when Leonardo da Vinci bought a consignment of Lefkara lace to decorate Milan Cathedral.

Cypriot copper- and silversmiths also had an international reputation and can still be seen at work in some of the handicraft centres, but the art is dying.

Overall, Cyprus is a fascinating mixture of Greek and Turkish cultures and then there are various refugees from around the Mediterranean, most notably Armenians and the Lebanese, all of whom have had an influence on Cypriot culture.

However, what might be of interest to British visitors are the remnants of the British colonial period. English theatre and films are available here, not least because the language is generally understood.

The influence of classical Greece (the art, literature and ceramics) and modern Greece and Turkey (the pop music and cuisine for starters) may be what is most apparent to first-time visitors to Cyprus. But for those who take the time to get to know the country, it becomes clear that Cyprus has a rich culture and strong identity that is all its own.

The dying art of the silversmith can be seen at craft centres throughout the island

Festivals and events

Cyprus's cultural calendar includes many traditional and religious festivals and events, in addition to the national days and political anniversaries. Many of the villages have folk festivals in summer and autumn, with displays of music, dance, flowers, embroidery and agricultural produce.

January

Fota (Epiphany) A public holiday, Fota is held every year on 6 January and is celebrated with religious services and events in the coastal towns. Traditionally, young men compete to find a crucifix thrown into the sea.

February–April

Apokreo (Carnival) This festival is held two weeks before the Greek Orthodox period of Lent, with the largest carnival taking place in Lemesos. It starts with Meat Week (Kreatini), which is the last chance to eat meat before Easter. There are parades and fancy-dress balls, especially in Lemesos.

Green Monday Green Monday signals the start of Lent and is traditionally celebrated with music and dancing. Again, Lemesos leads the way with elaborate fancy-dress parties, while in Pafos and Polis there are popular kite-flying competitions.

Easter The most important Greek Orthodox festival of the year, with the icon of St Lazarus being paraded through the streets of Larnaka.

May–July

Anthestiria (Flower Festival) The origins of this festival are in ancient Greece, where the god Dionysos was honoured. It also marks the rebirth of man and nature. It is usually held in May.

Kataklysmos (Festival of the Flood) Coinciding with Pentecost, 40 days after Easter, the origins of Kataklysmos lie in the destruction of earth's creatures in the great flood of biblical times. Ceremonies, music, dancing and a programme of water-based competitions take place in all the seaside towns.

Bellapaïs Music Festival Held in May and June, this festival has become one of the most important cultural events in north Cyprus. It centres on Bellapaïs Abbey where classical music fills the air and theatrical performances take place.

Larnaka International Summer Festival
With a mix of theatre, music and dance by artists from around the world, this festival has become one of Cyprus's foremost cultural events. Venues around Larnaka host different events. Held annually in July.

August–September

Assumption of the Virgin Mary Every year on 15 August Cyprus's monasteries and churches host celebrations for the Virgin Mary. They take the form of services and a gathering of families and villagers for feasting and dancing. It is a public holiday in Cyprus.

Lemesos Wine Festival During this 12-day annual festival in late August/early September, there is the opportunity to sample the best of Cyprus's wines. Every night, from 6pm to 11pm, the wine is offered free.

Agia Napa Festival This is held in Seferis Square, by the monastery, during the last week of September. The three-day programme includes theatre, opera, concerts and folk dancing.

October–December

Kyrenia International Olive Festival Held in mid-October to celebrate the olive harvest, this festival brings together all the townsfolk in a day of dancing, feasting on local delicacies and listening to music.

Christmas Christmas is celebrated with services, the gathering of family and friends, and much partying.

Christmas celebrations in Cyprus are always colourful

Festivals and events

Impressions

The first thing to strike a new visitor to Cyprus will often be the heat; stepping off the plane can seem like walking into a blast of hot air, especially if holidaying in the summer months. The second and not unrelated experience will be that of thirst. Visitors are likely to drink three times as much as at home, not out of a desire to overindulge, but out of a genuine thirst. As a result, do not expect, in summer, to be able to undertake any strenuous exercise while on holiday.

The airports can be busy, but streamlined procedures for foreigners make things relatively bearable, even when the holiday flights are arriving and departing at the same time. Huge numbers of taxis gather at the airports, usually distinctive and with worry beads hanging from the front mirror. These drivers believe speed is of the essence, and are masters of the art of finely judged overtaking.

Driving

For those preferring to trust their own driving skills, there is a multitude of car-hire firms at the airports and all around the resorts. Car-hire costs are fairly reasonable and good deals can be found on the Internet (*see pp177–8*).

Driving is on the left. The roads are generally good and well signposted. The dual carriageways, which link all main towns, make crossing the island faster. There are, however, still many stretches of single carriageway, where very slow-moving lorries can be encountered. The

towns can be busy, especially in the evening rush hour, and visitors should remember that Cypriot drivers have a cavalier attitude to the highway code.

Where to stay

Cyprus is well set up for the tourist, and hotels are of a very high standard. The independent traveller can get by, although not as cheaply as might be expected. 'Rooms to rent' are everywhere, and one of the first things that will strike you as you arrive at any town or village is just how many signs there are – they confront you at every corner. The island is lacking in budget hotels (there are few hostels) yet there are atmospheric small hotels and stylish boutique properties opening every year.

Mountains

All visitors who want to gain a complete picture of Cyprus should spend some time in the mountains. The Troodos Mountains are particularly high and provide a welcome escape from the heat of the plains. There are several villages with good hotels and restaurants; things to do include walking, birdwatching, mountain biking and exploring the Byzantine churches. With their labyrinthine streets, the mountain villages tumbling down the hillside have a distinctive charm worth savouring.

In winter visitors can enjoy the rare pleasure of a Mediterranean skiing holiday. There is usually snow on Mount Olympos from January to March.

The coast

The coastline of Cyprus is extremely varied with the most attractive areas around Pissouri and Polis. The southeast of the island, around Agia Napa, is a major tourist resort, catering to package tourists. It has lost its Cypriot character, and has turned rather ugly due to the profusion of clubs, pubs and theme parks.

The sandy beaches in this area are attractive but they have now become very crowded. The beaches around Lemesos (Limassol) and Larnaka are longer, and offer more room to move. Avoid the beaches in town. Pafos and its environs are busy areas, but quiet beaches can be found.

The towns of Lemesos and Larnaka cater for the tourist trade and boast excellent commercial centres and accommodation.

The region between Lemesos and Pafos has more sites of interest per kilometre than any other part of the island: a great number of museums, the medieval castle of Kolossi or the grand theatre of Kourion, taking in the ancient site of Palaepaphos,

Car and bike hire is available for those visitors who wish to explore the island

embrace some of the most important archaeological finds in the Mediterranean. An added bonus to a trip around this area is the spectacular coastline.

The main road passes some distinctive white cliffs with glorious photographic opportunities at Petra tou Romiou, where Aphrodite, goddess of love, is supposed to have sprung from the waves.

Pafos (Paphos) and the west

Pafos is a popular tourist resort; its impressive archaeological sites, such as the House of Dionysos and the Tombs of the Kings, see more visitors than ever before.

The northwest of the island has the most remote and arguably the most beautiful areas. One place of note is

Polis, an attractive town with rooms to rent, a chic luxury five-star hotel, charming stone hotels and a campsite on the beach. Beyond Polis to Pomos Point (Akra Pomou) are long stretches of sandy beach and fishing harbours.

Lefkosia/Lefkoşa (Nicosia)

Lefkosia, the island's capital, is a modern, sophisticated place, although within the walls the atmosphere of the old town is preserved among the narrow streets and dark shops.

The north

The north (Turkish-speaking Cyprus) has a different atmosphere from the south. Northern Lefkoşa (Nicosia) has the air of a Turkish bazaar; Girne is a pleasant harbour with a fort at one end, while, to the east, Gazimağusa is one of

The harbour at the popular resort of Pafos

TIPS FOR TRAVELLERS

Mosquitoes

While mosquitoes in Cyprus do not carry malaria they can still be a real pest. They are less prevalent on the coast than inland. Visitors should carry insect repellent and mosquito coils. Protect wrists and ankles in the evening and ensure the room is clear before going to bed.

Language

Many Cypriots speak English, although they will appreciate attempts to speak Greek or Turkish. The Cypriot attempt at written English can, however, be less than accurate.

Sunburn

Take care not to spend too long in the sun. The sun is at its height between 11am and 3pm when fewer than 60 minutes can cause severe sunburn.

---

the best-preserved Venetian towns in the Mediterranean. The Greek part of the town, Ammochostos, is modern. A buffer area, however, lies empty and ghostly, inaccessible to all but the military since the invasion of 1974.

The Cypriot and the tourist

The Cypriots make life easy for the holidaymaker; many speak English and the innate genial gregariousness of the people makes the foreigner feel at ease. Cypriots are masters of the tourist industry; they remember your name and will go out of their way to be helpful.

However, the Cypriots' warmth and friendliness can sometimes prove an annoyance to some Anglo-Saxons who may have a different concept of privacy. Female visitors travelling alone may also experience some old-fashioned

attention from older males that could be perceived as sexism.

There is also a certain tension between the liberal morality of visitors and that to which the Cypriots, or at least the Cypriot Church, are trying to cling. Older Cypriot women still keep themselves to themselves.

Cypriot life

To an extent Cypriots are bemused by foreigners. They do not share the passion for sun, sand and sea; most Cypriots spend their holidays in the mountains.

Cypriots seem happiest sitting in the café playing backgammon and discussing the intricacies of the political situation and whether the 'troubles' will ever be sorted out.

Village life

Life in the villages has changed little over the years, although modern ways are slowly having an impact. There are more than 300 villages on the island where traditional ways of life continue. Broadly speaking, Cypriot villages all seem to have the same plan of narrow roads and tracks converging into a central square.

The café is the fulcrum of the village, at least for the men, and is frequented at all times. Coffee is the preferred drink, a strong shot being served with a glass of water; the custom is to down it quickly. Later in the day, many switch over to brandy. *Tavli* or backgammon is a favourite pastime, and you will

The game *tavli* may not always be a cooling antidote for the afternoon sun

usually find a cut-throat game in progress.

Village women are clearly excluded from all this, but foreigners, male or female, are welcome. After the first curious glances the visitor is often left alone, but there may be an attempt to draw them into conversation. This is unlikely to be in English, but if you can't speak the language do not be deterred; there is something about Cypriot coffee shops that makes this ignorance almost irrelevant, especially after the inevitable ouzo or raki.

So what are the village women doing? It could well be that they do all the work, for even women of very mature years are seen on the outskirts of the village looking after the fields or tending donkeys piled high with straw and grasses. The men would undoubtedly point out, however, that they are early risers and have finished work by the time the tourist is taking breakfast: first light comes early to Cyprus's clear skies. They might also say that a visit to a shady backstreet will find their wives relaxing with their embroidery and knitting.

The quietness of the villages in the afternoon is always striking. One reason for this is that many young people leave to work in the towns and resorts, only coming back at the weekend when there will be a big gathering with all the family. At other times the village comes to life for a festival. A bandstand will be erected, and, on the appointed day, friends and relatives from the surrounding area gather to eat, drink and dance into the early hours.

The daily timetable

Business gets going earlier than visitors might be used to at home. Most offices are open by 8am. Then there is the siesta, that glorious peaceful period between 2pm and 5pm in summer, when the more sensible citizens are relaxing in the cool of their homes.

Things get going again around 5pm, and by 6pm it is pandemonium in most towns. Shops stay open until about 8pm and most Cypriots eat about 10pm or later, although restaurants are happy to serve you at any time of day. Despite their early start, Cypriots stay up late.

Expatriate life

Living in Cyprus – and many expatriates do set up transitory residence here – is on the one hand idyllic: the glorious days of summer, the relaxed way of doing things, the lack of crime and the reassuring similarity to life at home. But it also has its drawbacks: the relaxed way of doing things means that delivery will be promised tomorrow, and tomorrow will never come. The initial over-intimacy with local people may fade or remain frustratingly superficial, and there are basic differences of culture which cannot be ignored in a long stay. And curious as it may sound, it is even possible to become tired of going to the beach every weekend.

As a result, the expatriate community tends to set up its own groups and amusements. Few have much to do with the itinerant tourists, and the long-stay residents even tend to socialise together rather than with those who are only there for a couple of weeks.

Get up early and join the locals at a market

Lefkosia/Lefkoşa

Lefkosia (Nicosia) has been the capital of Cyprus since the 10th century. It sits on the Mesaoria Plain, with the rugged Beşparmak Mountains to the north and the eastern foothills of the Troodos Mountains to the south. The city, with a population of 313,000 in the south and 85,000 in the north, has expanded considerably in recent years, pushing into the surrounding orange groves and eucalyptus trees.

In high summer the midday heat numbs the brain, the temperatures being several degrees higher than on the coast. But around 5pm, meteorological factors combine to draw in a stiff breeze that brings relief, and at such times the tranquil atmosphere hides the reality that Lefkosia is a vibrant city with a bustling heart and a lively nightlife.

Partly because of the Green Line, the division between north and south, a sand-bagged border that slices Lefkosia in two, the walled town is a fascinating place. The streets are narrow and the buildings old, some crumbling, with many being renovated. The elevations in solid stone hide printing works and carpenters' shops, cobblers and a multitude of other trades. Interesting squares and palm-fringed open spaces punctuate the street pattern. For visitors, movement between the two sectors is allowed by way of the Ledra Palace and Ledra Street crossings (*see p15*).

Those who pass through the checkpoint may feel as if they have entered a different country, for the language is Turkish and the religion Muslim. The old town is the hub of a modern city. Outside the walls, multi-storey buildings and old colonial-style houses stand side by side, with shiny modern buildings going up all around.

Leoforos Archiepiskopou Makariou III is a wide street lined with banks, cafés, interior décor stores and smart boutiques. Further out there are hotels, embassies and residential neighbourhoods. The best place to view Lefkosia is from the **Ledra Museum and Observatory** (*Ledra St; tel: 22 679 369*), which offers superb vistas of the city. In the north, the old town is a charming place to explore with its old stone buildings and children playing in the squares.

History

The city was probably founded soon after the destruction of Constantia in the east in the 7th century. The impressive French Gothic buildings of Lefkosia date from when the island was acquired by a Frankish knight, Guy de Lusignan, in 1192. In 1489, the Venetians gained control of Cyprus, building the massive ramparts that we see today. In 1570 the Ottomans broke into the city after a six-week siege and Cyprus was soon entirely under their control. They ruled until 1878, when the island came under British administration. Partition of the city dates from 1964.

Greek-Cypriot Lefkosia
Agios Ioannis
(St John's Cathedral)

The first building on this site was a Benedictine abbey where, according to legend, the finger of St John the Baptist

See pp34–5 & 36–7 for walk routes

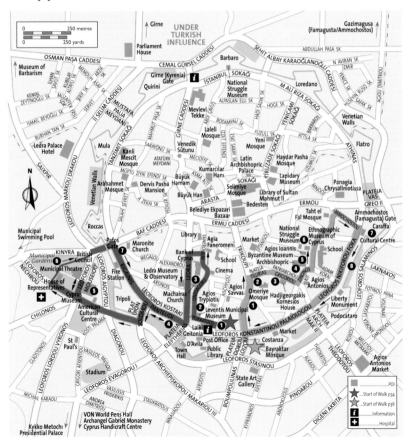

was preserved. However, this much-revered item was stolen by Mameluk raiders in 1426.

The current building dates from 1662 and the wall paintings have been restored and form an impressive collection.

Plateia Archiepiskopou Kyprianou, walled city. Open: Mon–Fri 8am–noon & 2–4pm, Sat 8am–noon. Free admission, but donations welcome.

Ammochostos (Famagusta) Gate

Originally one of the three main gateways through the old city walls, it was built in 1567 by a Venetian military architect, Giulio Savorgnano, who copied the design of a gate in Chania in Crete. To the rear is an open-air theatre which hosts the annual Nicosia Festival.

Leoforos Athinas. Tel: 22 430 877. Open: Oct–Apr Mon–Fri 10am–1pm, 4–7pm; May–Sept Mon–Fri 10am–1pm, 5–8pm.

Archangel Gabriel Monastery

The church of the monastery, which is set in lovely gardens, dates from the Byzantine era but was comprehensively rebuilt in the 17th century and then absorbed into the estate of Kykko Monastery. Inside there is a large fresco of the archangel, and, in the narthex, the tomb of the founder, Archbishop Nikiforos.

6km (4 miles) southwest of Lefkosia beside the Pediaios River. Open: daily.

Archbishop Makarios III Foundation Art Galleries

In the grounds of the centre, the Archbishop's Palace, or Archbishopric, is a huge mock-Venetian structure, which was started in 1956 but only completed years later. Not generally open to the public, on special occasions visitors can see the bedroom of Archbishop Makarios III, where his heart has been preserved. The centre has exhibitions and events open to the public.

Archbishopric, Plateia Archiepiskopou Kyprianou, walled city. Tel: 22 430 088. Open: Mon, Tue, Thur & Fri 8.30am–1pm & 3–5.30pm, Wed & Sat 8.30am–1pm. Free admission.

Byzantine Museum

This adjoins the grounds of the Archbishop's Palace, and was set up by the Archbishop Makarios III Foundation. The museum contains the largest collection of icons in Cyprus, dating from the 9th to the 18th centuries, and an art gallery displaying works from the 16th to the 19th centuries.

Archbishopric, Plateia Archiepiskopou Kyprianou, walled city. Tel: 22 430 008. Open: Mon–Fri 9am–4.30pm, Sat 9am–1pm. Admission charge.

Cyprus Museum

This archaeological museum has all the best finds from sites across Cyprus. Room 1 covers the Neolithic period and has a fine collection of soapstone idols. Also of interest in this room is the fragment of wall painting from Kalavasos, in which a headless man can just be made out.

Room 2 moves on to the Bronze Age, with a wide range of pottery and jugs. There are some relatively sophisticated depictions of animals and human figures.

Room 3 has finds from the late Bronze Age, including more pottery, showing a progression towards more advanced techniques. The middle case contains distinctive and much-copied examples of classical Greek pottery.

At the end of room 4, after various examples of pottery and sculpture, comes the finest exhibit in the museum: a case full of idols from a sanctuary at Agia Irini. The figurines are arranged as

they were found: a dazzling display of over 2,000 different shapes and sizes.

Rooms 5 and 6 form a sort of sculpture gallery. There is an extensive display of different figures from across a wide historical period.

Room 7 contains sculptures from the Roman period, including a huge naked representation of the Emperor Septimus Severus. In total contrast are some tiny, delicate figures in an adjacent case.

Further along are numerous bronze artefacts, knives and helmets. Of particular interest are the stamps and seals which are magnified so that visitors can see the detail. The Egyptian amulets are also worth closer inspection.

The Archbishop's Palace houses the preserved heart of Makarios III

To the right and downstairs are several sarcophagi, while upstairs are artefacts from ancient Salamis. Note especially the throne, the ivory chair, sections of a chariot and the huge bronze cauldron.

Back on the main corridor are paintings, jewellery and more sculpture. The final room has terracotta figurines from early religious sanctuaries.

Leoforos Mouseiou 1. Tel: 22 865 864. Open: Tue, Wed & Fri 8am–4pm, Thur 8am–5pm, Sat 9am–4pm, Sun 10am–1pm. Closed: Mon. Admission charge.

Ethnographic Museum of Cyprus

This museum of 19th- and 20th-century folk art is housed in the old Archbishopric, dating from the late 15th century. The buildings have been extensively restored.

The museum houses examples of wooden waterwheels, weaving looms, pottery, basketry, folk painting, woodcarving, metalwork, leatherwork, traditional costumes, embroidery, lace from Lefkara and textiles from the Karpaz, along with kitchen utensils and farming tools.

Plateia Archiepiskopou Kyprianou. Tel: 22 432 578. Open: Mon–Fri 9.30am–4pm. Closed: Sat & Sun. Admission charge.

Hadjigeorgakis Kornesios House

This is the house of Hadjigeorgakis Kornesios, the official interpreter and liaison (dragoman) to the Turkish governor between 1779 and 1809. It is a very fine example of 18th-century Turkish architecture, built around a courtyard with an impressive overhanging balcony. The house now contains the **Cyprus Ethnological Museum**.

The museum is upstairs in some very grand rooms. Visitors enter by a reconstructed living room and then tour the house anticlockwise. In the first room are documents (Hadjigeorgakis's letters and his translations). The second room explains the restoration of the house after it was bequeathed to the state by Hadjigeorgakis's last remaining descendants.

Further rooms contain paintings and sketches; family heirlooms, including sets of spoons, bronze utensils and weapons. A 19th-century dining room and bedroom have been reconstructed.

Patriarchou Grigoriou 20, walled city. Tel: 22 305 316. Open: Tue, Wed & Fri 8.30am–3.30pm, Thur 8.30am–5pm, Sat 9.30am–3.30pm. Closed: Mon & Sun. Admission charge.

Handicraft Centre

This is a state-run centre where local craftsmen can be seen making traditional items. The work ranges from weaving and woodcarving to pottery. Many items are for sale.

Leoforos Athalassas 186. Tel: 22 305 024. Open: Mon–Fri 7.30am–2.30pm, also Thur 3–6pm. Closed: Sat & Sun.

Kykko Metochi

This is an annexe of the Kykkos Monastery, which lies in the Troodos Mountains. The dependency contains quite extensive buildings and a church. It was built in the 19th century to facilitate the administration of the monastery's land.

Junction of Griva Digeni and Prokopiou.
Open: normally daily.
Free admission.

Laiki Geitonia

Laiki Geitonia means 'Local Neighbourhood' and this is a pedestrianised district just inside the old town. It contains several streets of restored houses, restaurants and shops. There are numerous souvenir shops and several good restaurants (*see also* Leventis Museum *below & p34*).
Between Plateia Eleftherias and Trikoupi, walled city.

Leventis Municipal Museum

This museum has been created in a restored 19th-century house. It was built in 1884 as a dowry for the daughter of a rich merchant but fell into disrepair. Demolition was

Reception room inside the Hadjigeorgakis Kornesios House

THE REVIVAL OF OLD LEFKOSIA

The government is subsidising the reconstruction of buildings in the old city, while maintaining traditional features and details. In fact, the effect can already be seen in the area near Ammochostos (Famagusta) Gate. The programme now covers areas outside the walls, including Kaimakli, Pallouriotissa and Agios Dhometios. The entire village of Fikardou has been declared an ancient monument (see p102).

imminent, when the Leventis Foundation stepped in to restore the building and establish this museum of Nicosia's history.

The museum is sophisticated; the exhibits are well laid out with audiovisual aids enhancing the display.

The exhibits cover 6,000 years of history, starting with artefacts from 4000 BC. The displays from the Lusignan and Venetian periods are particularly interesting, with examples of noblemen's costumes and early books which refer to Cyprus.

There is also an exhibition covering the period from British rule up to the present day. The early photographs of colonial Cyprus are very illuminating. There is a section covering the last 40 years, including an inevitably partial account of the fight for independence and of the 1974 troubles.

In the basement are a few more medieval artefacts and a small café.
Ippokratous 17, walled city.
Tel: 22 661 475. Open: Tue–Sun
10am–4.30pm. Free admission.

Municipal Gardens, aviary and Municipal Theatre

The Municipal Gardens are opposite the Cyprus Museum and provide a refreshing alternative to the sights and museums. Extensive and well tended, they contain several small ponds and an aviary. Fronting the gardens is the neoclassical Municipal Theatre where frequent performances, of both Greek drama and international productions, are staged.
Leoforos Mouseiou. Tel: 22 480 300.

National Struggle Museum

The museum displays documents from the 1955 to 1959 period, from the struggle for independence against the British, and from the later 1974 troubles. The exhibits include uniforms, weapons and other implements used by the EOKA guerrillas.
Plateia Archiepiskopou Kyprianou.
Tel: 22 305 878. Open: Mon–Wed & Fri
8am–2pm, Thur 3–5.30pm.
Closed: Jul & Aug afternoons.
Free admission.

Omeriye Mosque

This mosque started out as a Christian church – St Mary's. In 1571, after the Ottoman conquest of the island, the leading general Mustapha Pasha turned it into a mosque. A particularly tall and elegant minaret was added in the conversion of the mosque. At weekends local workers eat communal lunches in the courtyard. Visitors are welcome; women should cover their heads.
Trikoupi. Open: daily except prayer times.

Pafos Gate

This gateway was once one of the main entrances into the city. Today it is overlooked by UN troops. To enter the city by the Pafos Gate, visitors walk through the UN buffer zone separating the north and the south, the Green Line, which crosses the city.

The minaret of the Omeriye Mosque, named after a Muslim prophet

Presidential Palace

The original building on this site was constructed by the British, but it was burnt down during riots in 1931. A new residence was built and passed over to the president on Independence Day. The building was destroyed again in the coup of 1974, but, undeterred, the Cypriots restored it once more and it continues to be used as the presidential office.

Proedrikou Megarou, southwest suburbs of Lefkosia, 2.5km (1½ miles) from city centre. It is not open to the public.

Venetian walls

These are the most imposing structures in the city, and are remarkably well preserved, given that they were built in 1567. Initially, the walls took a wider circuit, but the Venetians narrowed it to 4.5km (2¾ miles). They built 11 bastions and three gates: Ammochostos, Pafos and Girne (*see p28, above, p35, p40 & p44*).

VON World Pens Hall

Opened by Vladimir Ouloupis Niros in 2004, this unique collection of writing instruments is housed in an attractive old mansion and contains pens made by jewellers such as Fabergé and Tiffany for monarchs and aristocrats.

Leoforos Demostheni Soveri 37. Tel: 22 463 204. Open: Jun–Sept Mon, Tue, Thur & Fri 9am–1pm & 4–8pm, Sat 9am–1pm; Oct–May Mon, Tue, Thur & Fri 9am–1pm & 3–7pm. Closed: Wed & Sun. Admission charge.

Walk: Greek western Lefkosia

This walk takes in the main shopping streets of Old Lefkosia and some of the historical points of interest and museums. It offers a chance to absorb some local culture too.

See the map on p27 for the route.

Allow 1 hour, or longer if the Cyprus Museum is visited.

Start at Laiki Geitonia, just inside the city walls.

1 Laiki Geitonia

This area of the city has been restored rather prettily to provide several pedestrianised streets of craft shops, traditional restaurants and the tourist office.

Turn on to Ippokratous, the main pedestrianised street of Laiki Geitonia, to find the Leventis Municipal Museum.

2 Leventis Municipal Museum

This museum has exhibits which tell the history of Lefkosia. It has three floors of interest: the first covers the city's early history up to Turkish rule; the ground floor, from British rule to independence; and there are some medieval artefacts in the basement.

Proceed towards Onasagorou and turn right. Continue into Faneromeni and eventually reach Agia Faneromeni Church. Turn left just before the church, and then left into Ledra St.

3 Ledra and Onasagorou streets

These two narrow streets were once the main shopping areas of Lefkosia. They are lined with a wide range of cafés and shops. The most notable shops are those selling ice cream and your typical high-street stores with global brands from Zara to Bershka.

Continue to the end of Ledra St, where it meets Plateia Eleftherias.

4 Plateia Eleftherias

This is a busy place with kiosks, fast-food outlets and, opposite, a bastion of the city walls. It is very much the heart of the city, standing as the gateway between the old and the new.

Turn right on Leoforos Kostaki Pantelidi, and then left into Plateia Dionysiou Solomou. From here cross over the walls and turn right into Leoforos Omirou, then head straight on. At the roundabout turn right into Leoforos Mouseiou. The museum is on the right.

5 Cyprus Museum

This houses one of the finest collections of archaeological treasures in the Mediterranean.

The first exhibits are objects from the Neolithic period, including a wall painting of a man with his hands up. Next comes the Bronze Age, followed by artefacts from the classical Greek period. At the end of room 4 is perhaps the most impressive display: a whole case of soapstone idols arranged as they were found in a sanctuary at Agia Irini.

The remaining rooms pass through the various periods of history. Don't miss the Salamis treasure upstairs.
Retrace your steps to the roundabout by the museum and turn right into Leoforos Nechrou and turn right again into the Municipal Gardens.

6 Municipal Gardens

Well-watered gardens full of trees, flowers, a few ponds and a small collection of sad-looking birds.
Leave the gardens at the Leoforos Mouseiou/Kinyra roundabout. Take the third exit, over which a UN flag flies, to reach Pafos Gate.

7 Pafos Gate

This used to be one of the main gateways into the city through the walls, but it has fallen into disrepair.
Turn uphill, keeping close to the walls, pass the fire station and eventually emerge back on to Plateia Eleftherias.

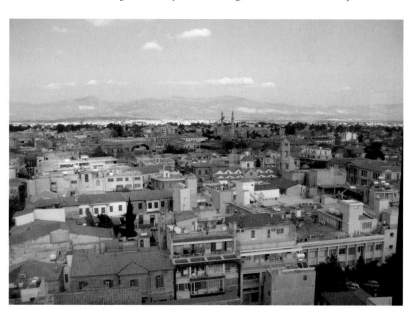

View over Lefkosia from the Ledra Street Observatory

Walk: Greek western Lefkosia

Walk: Greek eastern Lefkosia

This walk explores the sights within the walls of the eastern part of the city. Here you get a true sense of history.

See the map on p27 for the route.

Allow 1 hour, or longer if you visit any of the museums.

Start at Plateia Dorou Loizou and head into the old city down Trikoupi.

1 Trikoupi

Trikoupi is typical of the old city, narrow with even narrower pavements cluttered further by the overspill from shops and cafés. It is fairly shabby but has a certain charm.

The Omeriye Mosque is on the right, after about 200m (220yds).

2 Omeriye Mosque

Originally a church, this building was converted into a mosque by the Ottoman Turks to commemorate the Muslim prophet Omar, who was thought to have stayed here.

Turn right into Plateia Tillirias, and right again into Patriarchou Grigoriou, and after 100m (110yds) on the right is Hadjigeorgakis Kornesios House.

3 Hadjigeorgakis Kornesios House

The house is built around a courtyard and is a fine example of 18th-century Turkish architecture. The museum contains artefacts from the Turkish period (*see also p30*).

Turn left down Zinonos Kitieos to reach the Archbishop's Palace.

4 Archbishopric

The Archbishopric is a large mock-Venetian-style palace, generally closed to the public.

Continue past the Archbishopric to the adjacent Byzantine Museum and Agios Ioannis Church.

5 Byzantine Museum and Agios Ioannis Church

In the courtyard beside the Archbishopric is the Byzantine Museum with a fine collection of 9th- to 18th-century icons.

Agios Ioannis was built in 1662 and has a fine display of restored paintings on the ceiling and walls. The archbishops of Cyprus are enthroned here. The Ethnographic Museum (*see p30*) is next to Agios Ioannis.

Continue along the road to reach the National Struggle Museum on your left.

6 National Struggle Museum

This contains items relating to the fight for independence from Britain such as photographs, personal effects of heroes and memorabilia.

Continue northwards to a pedestrianised area. At the far end is the Taht el Fal Mosque, not open to the public. Turn right on to Ammochostou, and head for the Ammochostos Gate at the far end.

7 Ammochostos (Famagusta) Gate

This used to be one of the main entrances into the old city (*see p28*).
Turn right to follow the walls.

8 Venetian walls

The walls are perhaps the most impressive sight in Lefkosia, and stretch for 4.5km (2³/₄ miles) with 11 bastions.
Follow the road round the walls, passing the Bayraktar Mosque, then return to Plateia Dorou Loizou.

Ammochostos Gate, the finest Venetian monument in Lefkosia

Turkish-Cypriot Lefkoşa

Arabahmet Mosque
(Arabahmet Cami)

With its high minaret and large dome, the Arabahmet Mosque is a most dramatic place of worship. It was built by the Ottoman Turks in 1845 in memory of the conqueror of Cyprus, Arab Ahmet Pasha.

The courtyard contains a fountain and several tombs of statesmen, the most significant being that of the Grand Vizier, Kâmil Pasha. The mosque claims to preserve a

The high minaret of the Arabahmet Mosque, one of the most beautiful of the Ottoman period, rises above the town

hair from the Prophet's beard.
Salahi Şevket Sokağı.
Open: normally daily. Visits not permitted during prayer times.

Bedesten

The name *bedesten* means 'covered bazaar', and it reveals what became of this former Byzantine church after the Ottoman occupation of Cyprus.

It was built during the 12th century and was known as the Church of St Nicholas. With the arrival of the Ottomans it became a grain store and then a marketplace.

Above the grand north door are six Venetian coats of arms and in the highest part of the gable a delicate tracery can be seen. The building is, in fact, two churches of different periods, the southern half being the older. The medieval tombstones are thought to be from the Omeriye Mosque in Greek-Cypriot Lefkosia.
Arasta Sokağı by the Selimiye Mosque.
Open: normally daily. Free admission.

Belediye Ekpazari Bazaar

A huge covered market that marks the centre of old Lefkoşa. It sells fresh produce.
Arasta Sokağı. Open: Mon–Fri 7am–5pm, Sat 7am–2pm.

Büyük Hamam

This interesting building is unusual in that its former ground floor is now well below street level, a consequence of the surrounding area being filled and

In the Middle Ages, Büyük Han was part of a network of inns where merchants could rest

raised. Built in the 14th century as the Church of St George of the Latins, it was converted by the Ottomans into the baths which are still used today.
Mousa Orfenbey Sokağı. Open: Jun–Sept daily 9am–2pm; Oct–May daily 9am–1pm & 2–4.45pm. Free admission.

Büyük Han

The Han is one of the most impressive monuments built by the Ottomans on the island. It dates from 1572 and is attributed to Mustafa Paşa, the first Ottoman Governor of Cyprus. Its original purpose was as an inn with a small mosque. In 1893 it became Lefkoşa's central prison until in 1963 it was taken over by the Department of

Antiquities and restored. Inside is a lovely courtyard with bars, cafés and lots of little shops selling handicrafts, antiques and souvenirs.
Asma Alti Sokağı. Open: Mon & Thur 8am–7pm, Tue, Wed & Fri 8am–midnight, Sat 8am–4pm. Closed: Sun.

Dervis Pasha Mansion (Ethnographical Museum)

Dervis Pasha was the owner and editor of *Zaman*, the first Turkish-language newspaper in Cyprus. It was first published in 1891 and widely read, even in Turkey. The museum has two floors, the lower solidly built in stone; the upper level in mud bricks. This second floor was the main residence, the ground floor accommodating the servants and storerooms. For a long time the mansion was neglected. It was taken over by the Department of Antiquities in 1978 and restored.

One part of the building has been arranged as a bedroom, a dining room, bride's room and weaving room. The other section is set out as a living room. There is a courtyard, complete with flowerbeds and a pomegranate tree.
Beliğ Paşa Sokağı. Open: Tue–Sat, Jun–Sept 9am–7pm; Oct–May 9am–1pm & 2–4.45pm. Admission charge.

Girne (Kyrenia) Gate

When the Venetians built the defensive walls of the city they incorporated three entrances into the circular plan. These eventually became known as the Ammochostos, Pafos and Girne gates.

Girne Gate is the most northerly of the three and it was initially called Porta del Proveditore after the military architect Proveditore Francesco Barbaro. It was repaired by the Ottomans in 1821. The Arabic script on the large panel above the doorway includes verses from the Koran.

In 1931, the British cut new entrances into the city on either side of the gate, completely separating it from the walls. It now houses the tourist office.
At the meeting point of Girne Caddesi and Cemal Gürsel Caddesi.

Kumarcılar Hanı

This Ottoman inn, built at the end of the 17th century, has two floors, with Gothic arches supporting the upper floor and its roof of domes. There are 52 rooms in total. The upper floor housed the private hotel rooms, and the ground floor contained all the stores and servants' quarters. Since 1976 the building has been the head office of the Department of Antiquities.
Asma Altı Sokağı. Free admission.

Lapidary Museum

The building itself is an interesting 14th-century Venetian house. Inside is a display of stone carvings, many from the Selimiye Mosque. Perhaps the most remarkable exhibits are from the tomb of the Dampierre family and the 13th-century tombstone of Adana from Antioch. In the garden are the capitals from Corinthian columns, winged lions of St Mark and rose windows.
The garden wall has an interesting pointed arch with astonishing gargoyles on either side. Various heraldic shields are carved out of the wall itself.

If the museum is shut, knock on the door of the custodian of the Library of Sultan Mahmut II, across the way by the Selimiye Mosque, and they will let you in.
Kirlizade Sokağı. Open: Tue–Sat, Jun–Sept 9am–2pm; Oct–May 9am–1pm & 2–4.45pm. Admission charge.

Latin Archbishopric Palace

The building dates from 1329, although the upper storey was rebuilt in 1571 by the first Ottoman chief-kadi who lived there. At one time it was the governor's

house. The upper storey is ornamented with carved timber shelves. In one of the rooms there is an interesting carved wooden niche, finished in various colours; the ceiling is also worthy of examination. This room would have been the main reception area.
Northeast end of the Selimiye Mosque.

Library of Sultan Mahmut II

This small building, known as the Eaved House, was built by the Ottoman governor in 1829. The collection of oriental books includes several richly ornamented Korans and some excellent examples of Turkish and Persian calligraphy. At ceiling level, all around the walls, is a gilded inscription in blue and gold written in honour of the sultan by the Turkish-Cypriot poet Müftü Hilmi. If the custodian is not present, try the Lapidary Museum across the street.
Kirlizade Sokağı. Open: Tue–Sat, Jun–Sept 9am–2pm; Oct–May 9am–1pm & 2–4.45pm. Admission charge.

The Latin Archbishopric Palace

Mevlevi Tekke (Turkish-Cypriot Ethnographic Museum)

This museum, founded in 1962, is housed in the 16th-century tekke of the Dervish sect of the Mevlevi religious order, and in this very building they would perform their famous whirling dance. A tekke is the Muslim equivalent of a Christian monastery.

It is a fascinating place with a musicians' gallery looking down on where the Dervishes whirled. There are many exhibits of musical instruments, costumes, embroidery and metalwork.

Adjoining the museum is a long mausoleum with a line of 15 tombs, resting places of Dervishes who had held important posts in the tekke. Out in the yard are several other tombstones.

Girne Caddesi. Open: Mon–Fri, Jun–Sept 9am–2pm; Oct–May 9am–1pm & 2–4.45pm.
Admission charge.

National Struggle Museum

An exhibition of weapons and newspaper cuttings portrays the struggle of the Turkish Cypriots in the face of the Enosis (Union with Greece) threat up to 1974 and the atrocities committed.

Mucahiddin Complex on the Barbaro Bastion. Open: Tue–Sat, Jun–Sept 9am–2pm; Oct–May 9am–1pm & 2–4.45pm. Admission charge.

Selimiye Mosque (Selimiye Cami)

The Lusignans left an impressive legacy of ecclesiastical buildings. Hosting great Muslim festivals like Bayram, the Selimiye Mosque, formerly the Cathedral of Santa Sophia until 1954, is one of the most impressive monuments of Christian architecture in the Near East, and it is little wonder that the Lusignan royalty considered it a fitting place to crown their kings.

Started in 1208, the building was consecrated more than a century later in 1326. Even then work continued for many decades and the towers of the west front were never fully completed. The building was ransacked by the Genoese in 1373 and by the Mameluks 50 years later. It was also damaged by earthquakes, the one in 1547 leading to the east-end clerestory being rebuilt by the Venetians.

The work of the original French craftsmen is especially fine in the west front, in the central portal and the great window above. A series of impressive flying buttresses forms part of the

MUSLIM CONVERSION

After the Ottomans entered Lefkosia in 1570 they proceeded to convert the Cathedral of Santa Sophia into a mosque. In accordance with Muslim tradition, every reproduction of the human form had to be removed. All the interior tombstones were either removed or used to pave the floor. A collection of them can be seen today in a small chamber beside the mosque. The tall minarets were added some time later.

complex nave and these continue to some effect around the semicircular apse at the east end.

Within the building are massive cylindrical columns with marble capitals. The Turkish Cypriots added a *mihrab* (a vaulted niche) and *minbar* (pulpit), features of all mosques. A *gibla* indicates the direction of Mecca, and the carpets are arranged diagonally with this orientation in mind.

Selimiye Sokağı. Open: normally daily except prayer times. Visitors must be modestly dressed.

The Selimiye Mosque's beautiful vaulted ceiling

Walk: Turkish-Cypriot Lefkoşa

For those staying in the southern side of the island this walk will give them an insight into the island's history and into the different culture and perspective of Turkish-Cypriot Cyprus. Those on holiday in the north will find this a useful way of exploring Lefkoşa.

Allow 1 hour.

From Pafos Gate follow Leoforos Markou Drakou north to the checkpoint at the old Ledra Palace Hotel.

1 Checkpoint

The border is open 24 hours. There are formalities for both sets of authorities, so be prepared to wait.

Walk through the Greek-Cypriot checkpoint into the UN buffer zone, complete the formalities at the Turkish-Cypriot checkpoint, then head straight on to the roundabout where you should turn right to follow the line of the city walls. Turn into the old city at Girne (Kyrenia) Gate.

2 Girne (Kyrenia) Gate

This used to be one of three gateways into the old city, built by the Venetians. The Ottomans added to it but the British decided it was too narrow, and built a new entrance. The old gateway now stands in the middle of the road now housing the tourist office, while the traffic passes on either side.

Go into the city on Girne Caddesi, and after 100m (110yds) on the left is the Mevlevi Tekke.

3 Mevlevi Tekke

This 17th-century building was the home of the Whirling Dervishes, an Islamic sect from Turkey, who whirled in a distinctive dance on the stage. It is now an ethnographical museum.

Continue down Girne Caddesi for a further 200m (220yds) to reach Atatürk Meydanı.

4 Atatürk Meydanı (Atatürk Square)

Atatürk was the founder of modern Turkey, and statues of him can be found all over northern Cyprus. The Venetian column in the centre of the square is a much older monument. The Hotel Saray is here.

Bear left with the road, and then take the first direct right, using the twin minarets of the Selimiye Mosque as a landmark. Follow the first right for the Turkish Bath.

5 Büyük Hamam (Turkish Bath)

This was originally a Christian church (St George of the Latins) but was converted to a Turkish bath which is still used today. The proprietor will show you round, leading you from the cool of the fountain house into progressively hotter rooms. Better yet, take time out to enjoy a hammam.
Turn right out of the bath, then right again until the turrets of Büyük Han come into view ahead.

6 Büyük Han

Built in 1572, Büyük Han was formerly an Ottoman inn with two storeys of rooms and an octagonal mosque in the square. It has been carefully restored and its charming cafés make a great rest stop.
Turn left on Arasta Sokağı and follow it round to reach the Selimiye Mosque.

7 Selimiye Mosque

This was originally the Cathedral of Santa Sophia, built in 1208, and was the most imposing building in Lefkoşa (*see pp42–3*). It is now a mosque, and is used daily for prayers. Visitors can enter if they are dressed modestly, although not during prayer times.

Beyond the mosque are the sultan's library and the Lapidary Museum.

8 Lapidary Museum

Situated in a 14th-century Venetian house, it is thought that this building was in the courtyard of the Cathedral of Santa Sophia and was used as accommodation by pilgrims. The museum has a display of stone carvings and architectural features that have fallen off buildings.
Take the path that goes round the south side of the mosque, passing the Bedesten. Back on Arasta Sokağı, turn right past Büyük Han. On the right at the crossroads is Kumarcılar Hani.

9 Kumarcılar Hanı

This also used to be an inn, and now has shops built into its walls. The owner of the café will let you through to the courtyard.
Bear right around the Hanı, and then take the road to the north, Akiah Efendi Sokağı, then left to reach Atatürk Meydanı, 100m (110yds) further on.

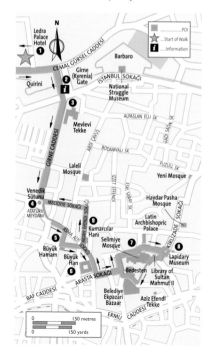

The southeast

This section takes in the lower slopes of the eastern Troodos and the flat lands that reach to the seas of Gazimağusa Bay. The coastal boundaries of the area run past Akra Petounta (Petounda Point) to the town of Larnaka before sweeping around the bay to Cape Pyla and on to spectacular Cape Gkreko, turning north to Protaras (Fig Tree Bay).

Around Larnaka the landscape is white and arid, a very striking terrain when viewed from the heights of nearby Stavrovouni Monastery. The desert landscape does relent, however, but not until the eastern shores of Larnaka Bay. Here, the soil is a rich red, and with the good weather conditions and efficient irrigation an early crop of vegetables for export is assured.

Much of the coastline west of Larnaka is equally picturesque even at Cape Kiti, where holiday development is now established. Larnaka Bay is fringed with large modern hotels and the beaches have been improved as a result.

It is not until the Agia Napa coast that sandy beaches are found. Here, a turquoise sea washes over fine, light-coloured sand. Unfortunately, it is a very popular area now, with new developments spoiling what was once a picturesque environment.

A little way along the coast, beyond the villa development of Protaras, and plainly visible from Deryneia (Dherinia), is the holiday town of Varosha, a suburb of Gazimağusa, which stands deserted in stark contrast to the overflowing resorts to the south, closed off since the division. Gazimağusa's commercial centre, on the other hand, is a bustling university town with a beautiful old town.

LARNAKA

Larnaka is the main town of the area and plays a prominent part in

'The affinity of the landscape is with Asia rather than the other Greek islands. The earth is bleached to whiteness; only a green patch of vines or flock of black and tawny goats relieves its arid solitude … And over the whole scene hangs a peculiar light, a glaze of steel and lilac, which sharpens the contours and perspectives, and makes each vagrant goat, each isolated carob tree, stand out from the white earth as though seen through a stereoscope.

'The prospect is beautiful in the abstract, but violent and forbidding as the home of man.'
ROBERT BYRON, *The Road to Oxiana*, 1937

commercial life. It has expanded considerably in recent years with new residential development, resulting in a virtual maze of identical streets.

During its history, the town has seen many changes, and in 1974 it suddenly acquired an airport, which placed it strategically on the tourist route. Modern-day tourism is a way of life for the people of Larnaka, but some still remember a holiday trade of a different kind, when it was popular with the staff of foreign consuls.

History

The town is built on the ancient site of Kition, an important city of antiquity dating from the 13th century BC. It was a location crippled by earthquakes and consequently the city fell into decline a mere 300 years after its foundation.

During Roman and Byzantine times Kition was not of significance and, with the coming of Lusignan rule, the name Salinas related it to the nearby salt lake.

The name Larnaka came into use during the second half of Ottoman rule when the town once again became a centre of trading in the Levant and a popular port of embarkation for Christian pilgrims on their way to the Holy Land.

The southeast

Larnaka (Larnaca) *(see pp52–3 for walk route)*

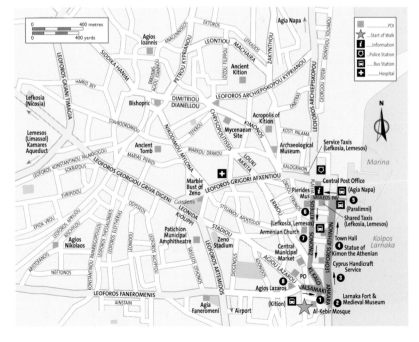

Agios Lazaros

This interesting church owes its name and prominence to events preceding the present construction. Legend states that Lazarus, the brother of Mary and Martha, was resurrected by Jesus at Bethany in Palestine and promptly expelled by the Jews. He definitively died in Cyprus and was buried in a church that stood on the present site and was renamed after him. In 890 his tomb was discovered, and some time later his body was stolen only to reappear, first in Constantinople, and then in Marseille. In the 17th century the church was rebuilt and the impressive campanile added.

Four domes cover the central nave, although they are underdrawn and not visible from below. The main roof is supported on four massive double piers, a rococo pulpit being ingeniously designed into one of them, while another supports a 17th-century icon depicting the death of Lazarus. Also of note is the iconostasis, an 18th-century woodcarving, and by the south entrance, the doors carry Byzantine and Lusignan coats of arms. In the south apse the saint's empty sarcophagus can be seen.
Junction of Agiou Lazarou and Leoforos Faneromenis. Tel: 24 652 498.
Open: Apr–Aug daily 8am–12.30pm & 2–6.30pm; Sept–Mar daily 8am–12.30pm & 2–5.30pm. Free admission.

The 17th-century campanile at Agios Lazaros

Ancient Kition

Most of the ancient city lies buried under the modern town. Over the years three areas of interest have been discovered, and many of the artefacts from these sites can be seen in the **Archaeological Museum** (*see p50*). The **Acropolis** dates from the 13th century BC. It stood on Bamboula Hill, perhaps with an open-air theatre. In 1879, before it was realised that the area had archaeological importance, the British army razed much of the hill. There is very little to be seen today.

The fascinating ruins of ancient Kition, the city which was allegedly founded by Noah's grandson Khittim; excavations of the site continue to this day

Mycenaean site

As with the acropolis, not a great deal survives. However, in 1962 and 1963, a treasure of pottery, ornaments, jewellery and alabaster vessels was discovered in tombs by a courtyard. Later, a number of workshops for making copper implements were uncovered.

KIMON KITEOS THE ATHENIAN

'Though dead, he was victorious.'
So translates the inscription below the marble bust of Kimon, a Greek general.

In 450 BC he laid siege to Kition with 200 ships in an attempt to help the Cypriot kings rid themselves of Persian domination. Kition supported the Persian cause, and Kimon was felled in action. As he lay dying, he sounded the retreat and his ships sailed away. The marble bust is prominently located on the seafront along Leoforos Athinon.

Main site

Now surrounded by housing, this is the most extensive of the three sites, and visitors will obtain a good view of the excavations from a raised wooden gantry. This part of Kition lies by the ancient city's north wall. The latter was built out of mud bricks with more substantial bastions in limestone. They date from the 13th century BC. One hundred years later the Mycenaeans came to this coast and superimposed massive structures on the earlier walls. The remains of a large temple can be seen, which in the 9th century BC the Phoenicians converted into a temple to Astarte. Several other temples have been discovered in recent years.

Surprisingly, little evidence of Hellenistic and Roman involvement, so prominent in other parts of Cyprus, is to be found.

The acropolis site is located halfway along Kimonos, with the Mycenaean site at the northern end. Both sites are unsupervised. The main site is further north and approached from Leontiou Machaira. The main site is open: Mon–Wed & Fri 8am–2.30pm, Thur 8am–5pm. Closed: Sat & Sun. Admission charge for the main site.

Archaeological Museum

The museum houses many relics unearthed from the excavations at Kition. The ceramic artefacts are especially interesting. However, not all the objects are from Kition, and there is a fascinating presentation of limestone torsos, heads and terracotta figurines. On the upper floor, a section of the museum illustrates how the Neolithic inhabitants of Khirokitia lived and were buried. Out in the garden there is a mass of incomplete statues. The museum also houses a marble bust of Zeno.

Larnaka Fort was erected in 1625 by the Ottoman Turks

ZENO, THE STOIC

Larnaka had a most distinguished citizen in Zeno, the founder of Stoic philosophy, or so it is claimed in Larnaka. Zeno was a celebrity and a Phoenician, not a Greek. He was born in Kition in 333 BC, but left in 313 to study philosophy in Athens. His marble bust, at the western end of Leoforos Grigori Afxentiou, is a copy of the only existing statue of Zeno in the museum at Herculaneum in Italy. It was erected in 1921 by the Pierides family in honour of a relative, Zeno Demetrios Pierides (1811–95).

Plateia Kalograion. To the north of the town centre at the junction of Kilkis and Kimonos. Tel: 24 304 169. Open: Tue–Wed & Fri 8am–3pm, Thur 8am–5pm, Sat 9am–3pm. Closed: Mon & Sun. Admission charge.

Kamares Aqueduct

The name means 'the Arches', and the massive arched watercourse was built by the Ottoman Turks in 1745 to bring water to Larnaka from wells on the River Trimithius.

Altogether, there were three sections, giving a total of 75 arches, but today only 33 remain. The tremendous structure, which dominates the outskirts of the town, was in use until 1930. It is illuminated at night.
3km (2 miles) outside Larnaka on the road to Lemesos (Limassol).

Larnaka Fort and Medieval Museum

This building was erected by the Ottomans in 1625. It became well known to the visiting warships of Christian countries; they were obliged to fire a salute on anchoring and then await a reply from the cannons of the fort. A certain amount of patience was needed, for this was by order of the governor in Lefkosia and had to be obtained by messenger. The cannon ports can still be seen today.

In later times the fort was used by the British as a prison, and the remains of the gallows are to be found near the door. It now houses exhibits from Kition and Hala Sultan Tekke. Occasionally, in summer, the open courtyard is fitted out with seats for folk-dancing performances.

On the seafront at the south end of Ankara St. Tel: 24 304 576. Open: Jun–Aug Mon–Fri 9am–7.30pm; Sept–May Mon–Fri 9am–5pm. Closed: Sat & Sun. Admission charge.

Patichion Municipal Amphitheatre

This open-air amphitheatre comes into its own during the Larnaka Festival in July, when there are concerts and performances of ancient Greek drama. Various events are also held in August. *Take the side road off the west side of Leoforos Artemidos, south of the turning to Lemesos (Limassol), opposite the Cyprus Popular Bank. Open: only for performances.*

Pierides Museum

The collection was begun in 1839 by Demetrios Pierides, a man of Venetian ancestry, although the museum wasn't opened until 1974. Six generations of his family have continued his work, and today there are 3,600 objects from various periods of Cyprus's history. The remarkable male nude of the Chalcolithic period is worth a second glance, as is the long-necked woman of 325–50 BC. There is a display of Roman glass and some interesting examples of early attempts at mapping the island.

The museum building was the home of Pierides, and its elevations are from the mid-19th century. The property used to be shared with the Swedish Consulate, a link going back to when Pierides was the honorary consul. *Zinonos Kitieos 4. Tel: 24 814 555. Open: Mon–Thur 9am–4pm, Fri–Sat 9am–1pm. Closed: Sun. Admission charge.*

This 19th-century building houses the Pierides Museum

NEARBY

There is a little garden outside the tourist office, dedicated to an EOKA guerrilla. It provides a useful place to escape the burning sun and rest the legs. It is located at Plateia Vasileos Pavlou, on the north end of Leoforos Athinon.

Walk: Larnaka

This walk explores the main tourist and shopping areas of Larnaka.

Allow 1 hour.

See the map on p47 for the route.

Start 100m (110yds) inland from the fort at the grand mosque of Larnaka.

1 Al-Kebir Mosque
One of several mosques in this part of Larnaka, it is still in use. Prayer times are posted outside, but it is open to visitors outside those times.
Head towards the seafront, and the fort.

2 Larnaka Fort
Built by the Ottoman Turks as a fort in 1625, this structure has since been used as a prison, and is now a museum, with exhibits from the site of Kition. Visitors may wish to exploit its seafront position and refresh their feet in the lapping waters.
Head north from the fort, along the coastal road, passing a number of cafés along the way.

3 Larnaka Beach
Larnaka's beach attracts many visitors from those looking for a swim or a game of beach volleyball.
Either walk along the beach, if it is not too crowded, or keep to the lively, palm tree-lined promenade. After you've gone about 200m (220yds), on the right of the road, you'll see the statue of Kimon the Athenian.

4 Kimon the Athenian
Kimon was one of the greatest heroes of early Cypriot history. He led a fleet of 200 triremes against the Persians but was killed in the ensuing battle. Those with troubles reputedly consult the statue for advice.
Continue along the road, and turn right towards the sea on Vasileos Pavlou. Walk along the breakwater.

5 Marina/Sea wall
The marina is fenced off to everyone except those who have boats moored here. However, there is a pleasant walk that goes along the boulders of the breakwater which is also a good place to swim from.
Turn inland on a busy stretch of road to Plateia Vasileos Pavlou, where the tourist office can be found. Turn left

into *Zinonos Kitieos, and after*
100m (110yds) on the right is the
Pierides Museum.

6 Pierides Museum

This 19th-century house with grey
shutters contains an extensive collection
of archaeological finds, maps and
folkloric artefacts that belong to the
Pierides family.
Continue along Zinonos Kitieos.

7 Zinonos Kitieos

This is the main shopping street in
Larnaka. The yellow building set
back from the road near Chrysios dress
shop is the Armenian Church and
school. There is a large Armenian
community in Cyprus who fled from
Turkey in 1896.

A confusing crossroads confronts the
walker at the end of Zinonos Kitieos.
Cross straight over and turn left into
Kleanthous Kalogera. At the next
crossroads take a sharp right and follow
the road round into Valsamaki to see
Agios Lazaros directly ahead.

8 Agios Lazaros

Built in the 9th century, the church has
a distinctive white-painted belfry. It
commemorates Lazarus who, legend
has it, was raised from the dead and
became the Bishop of Larnaka.

The church is surrounded by
peaceful cloisters, and is closed in the
early afternoon.
Proceed towards Valsamaki, but take the
first right, followed by the first left to
return to the fort and seafront.

Peaceful cloisters at Agios Lazaros in Larnaka

LARNAKA ENVIRONS
Agia Ekaterina (Royal Chapel)

This church is also well known as Pyrga Church. It was built in 1421, and is an interesting vaulted structure, although somewhat plain in appearance. Inside, the ribs of the vaults are painted with the badges of the House of Lusignan, and there are some murals, among them *The Last Supper* and *The Passing of Lazarus*. Enquiries for the key should be made at the coffee shop nearby.

In Pyrga village, 25km (16 miles) west of Larnaka. Open: daily at reasonable hours. Admission charge.

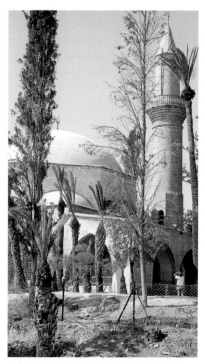

Hala Sultan Tekke near Larnaka – a place of pilgrimage

Hala Sultan Tekke
(Mosque of Umm Haram)

This tekke is set splendidly among the palm trees on the west bank of the salt lake, an oasis in the blistering heat of the salt flats.

It is here that Umm Haram, said to be the maternal aunt of the Prophet Muhammad, is buried. According to Muslim tradition, she was accompanying Arab raiders in AD 649 when she fell from her mule and broke her neck. She was buried on the spot and two huge stones were erected by the grave, with a third laid across the top.

It is an important place of Muslim pilgrimage, surpassed only by the shrines of Mecca, Medina and Al-Aqsa (Jerusalem). During the Ottoman occupation of Cyprus, all Turkish vessels had to lower their flags in homage as they sailed along the coast. Now the sanctuary is enclosed by a domed mosque built in 1816. Green cloth, a symbol of peace, is draped over the great stones.

Outside, a restored minaret stands as tall as the palm trees and overlooks the shady garden with its fountain and watercourse.

West bank of Larnaka's salt lake, on the road to Kition. First turning right after the airport, travelling south.
Open: Apr, May, Sept & Oct daily 8am–6pm; Jun–Aug daily 8am–7.30pm; Nov–Mar daily 8am–5pm. Free admission. Dress modestly.

Scenic splendour beyond the chapel at Moni Stavrovouni

Kition Tower

This modest construction is not in the village of Kition but stands to the southeast, about 300m (330yds) from the sea. The tower was built by the Venetians as an observation post and has been restored from a crumbling ruin. The bones of pigmy hippos were found in the floor.

5km (3 miles) southeast of Kition village and can be approached from Meneou or Perivolia. The last 400m (440yds) must be covered on foot.

Moni Stavrovouni (Stavrovouni Monastery)

The monastery can be seen from miles around as it is perched on top of a hill, standing in magnificent isolation 690m (2,264ft) above sea level.

Once through the gate the views over Larnaka and the Troodos Mountains are breathtaking. The buildings themselves are unimpressive. Parts date from the 17th century, but most sections are more recent, although erected on earlier foundations.

The monastery was built on the orders of St Helena, the mother of Constantine the Great. In AD 327, on her way back to Constantinople from Jerusalem, where she had found the True Cross, she landed in Cyprus and donated a fragment of the Cross to the foundation of the monastery. *Stavros* is Greek for 'cross', hence the name Stavrovouni.

It is claimed the fragment is still within the monastery, covered by a silver casing set into another cross, 500 years old, draped in damask. No one can be sure that it is the sacred relic, as the Arabs destroyed much of the monastery in 1426, and the Ottoman Turks set fire to the remainder in 1570. However, the

Panagia Angeloktistos in Kition village

monks claim that the holy relics survived the attack. Many of the monks have been here all their lives and produce some of the best honey in Cyprus.

Deep in the monastery's interior resides a macabre collection of skulls. At the lifting of a shutter the sun's rays pick them out with startling clarity. They are the skulls of dead monks, stacked on shelves, each with his name carved into his forehead.

40km (25 miles) west of Larnaka, off the Lefkosia–Lemesos Rd. Open: Apr–Aug daily 8am–noon & 3–6pm; Sept–Mar daily 8am–noon & 2–5pm. Only men may visit.

Panagia Angeloktistos

Although Angeloktistos means 'built by angels', all the evidence suggests that ordinary mortals constructed this church in the 11th century on the ruins of a 5th-century basilica. It was subsequently restored in the 16th

century. The building is in good shape, and a lantern dome crowns the crossing of the high central nave and transepts. A Latin chapel was added in the 13th century and it is now used as a narthex. Many of the icons as well as the iconostasis (screen) have been repainted and ruined to some extent, the large Archangel Michael at the right of the entrance surviving these assaults better than others. Above the main porch are three coats of arms.

The showpiece of the church is its mosaic, arguably the finest in Cyprus. It is situated in the central apse and can be illuminated for visitors. Angels attend the Virgin as she stands on a jewelled footstool, her left arm holding the Christ Child. On either side are the archangels Gabriel and Michael. Historians cannot agree on the date of this remarkable design, but it is older than the church, possibly 6th century.

Kition village, 9.5km (6 miles) southwest of Larnaka, off the road to Mazotos. Closed for restoration at the time of writing.

Salt lake

This remarkable phenomenon is several kilometres long and about 1.6km (1 mile) wide. In the summer it completely evaporates and is a place of great heat, the air shimmering above the white precipitate. The salt that forms on the surface is no longer collected. In winter, after as little as one day's rain, the scene is transformed when water covers the salty crust. Pink flamingos, escaping the cold of eastern Europe, make the lake their home for several months. They spend all their time in the middle, so binoculars are a necessity.

Geologists explain that the seawater from the adjacent shore passes through the porous rock and is trapped, where it forms a shallow lake below sea level. There is a similar salt lake on the Akrotiri Peninsula near Lemesos. *South of Larnaka. The airport road runs alongside a section of it.*

The beautiful mosaic depicting the Virgin and Christ Child at Panagia Angeloktistos

AGIA NAPA

This town was for a long time the centre of the holiday industry in the southeast, although the sprawling villa development of Protaras on the east coast has taken the lead. Agia Napa has a reputation for cheap beer, clubs and bars.

The original village centre, by the monastery, is attractive, but elsewhere there is a crowd of bars, cafés and clubs that come alive in the evening. Apart from the monastery, everything is new, and the streets are lined with souvenir shops, all selling the same goods. On the south side of the central square, heading west on Leoforos Kryou Nerou, is the **Thalassa Municipal Museum of the Sea** (*tel: 23 816 366; open: Jun–Sept Mon 9am–1pm, Tue–Sun 9am–1pm & 6–10pm, Oct–May Mon 9am–1pm, Tue–Sat 9am–5pm, closed: Sun*) and its displays of fossils and shells from Cyprus's waters.

Below the town, the small harbour with its seafood restaurants is constantly busy with boat and fishing trips. The beaches are good and prove a major attraction. At the east end, the sea has sculpted some incredible cliff formations, ideal for exploring by canoe.

Agia Napa Monastery

Entry to the monastery is off the village square. It was built by the Venetians in 1570, with massive, almost blank, external walls in contrast to the interior. This is a blessing today, for the outside can be a noisy place, but once through the arched doorway into the cloistered courtyard, all is calm. There are some finely carved windows, but the centrepiece of the courtyard is an octagonal fountain with four columns carrying a large dome. On each side is a high relief of garlands, coats of arms and animals' heads. To the north of the courtyard there is another unusual fountain, with water gushing out of a stone boar's head.

Part of the church building is underground, cut into the rock and entered by a flight of steps.

Sunset at Agia Napa, once a quiet fishing village, now a tourist centre

Golden sands and watersports at Protaras

Town centre by Plateia Seferi.
Open: normally daily.

Nissi Beach

The Nissi Beach Hotel overlooks the shore, which means a crowded beach in summer. Nevertheless, it is a fine stretch of white sands, edged by turquoise seas. The rocky island just offshore can be reached by wading, swimming or paddling. A few hundred metres to the east is a little inlet, ideal for bathing, called Sandy Bay. One and a half kilometres (1 mile) to the west of Nissi Beach is the equally enticing **Golden Sands**, a popular place, where soaring paragliders look down on the sunbeds.
2km (1¼ miles) west of Agia Napa.

Paralimni

This village has grown in recent years to accommodate some of the displaced population of Greek-Cypriot Famagusta. It is close enough to the holiday beaches to be influenced by tourism; in fact, there is a ribbon of development reaching to the distant shore. Nevertheless, it still pursues some of its market-gardening activities.

A modern open-air amphitheatre has been built and is used to promote cultural events in the area.
15km (9 miles) north of Agia Napa.

Potamos

Greek for 'river', this is a lovely little creek where numerous fishing boats tie up. There are cafés on the bank where the fishermen relax.
5km (3 miles) east of the village of Xylofagou.

Protaras (Fig Tree Bay)

Named after the fabled fig tree brought from the East, Fig Tree Bay or Protaras is a full-grown holiday resort with miles of hotels, villas, apartments, bars and restaurants. The perpetually crowded beach is good for swimming; the sand shelves gently into the clear blue sea. A little way out is a small rocky island. Because the waters generally stay calm the area is attractive to waterskiers. The runs down the coast are quite splendid.
East coast, 14km (9 miles) from Agia Napa via Cape Gkreko.

Walk: Agia Napa

Agia Napa has developed into one of the most popular tourist resorts. This walk explores parts of that area but also the attractive area along the coast.

Allow 2 hours.

Start at the village square.

1 Plateia Seferi (Seferis Square)

The large square in front of the monastery hosts stalls selling souvenirs and jewellery. During the Agia Napa festival, music and dance performances take place in the square.

Enter the monastery courtyard.

2 Moni Agia Napa (Monastery)

The monastery is by far the most impressive sight in Agia Napa. It is a peaceful place, now used as a conference centre. The monastery was supposedly founded by a Venetian noblewoman on the site of a cave where an icon of the Virgin Mary had been found. The building was restored in 1950.

Pass through the monastery courtyard, and out through an archway on to a path. This leads on to a tarred road heading to the sea. When it meets the main coast road, turn left to reach a cemetery, and then right to the harbour.

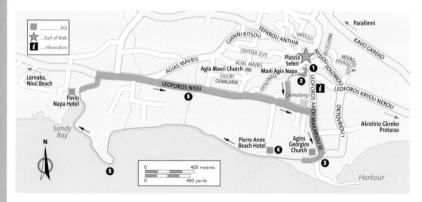

3 Harbour

The harbour retains some character despite the bars, cafés and shops around it. Small fishing boats are moored here and tourist boats take visitors on cruises to the surrounding area. The long beach is fine and sandy, although it gets crowded.

Take the path to the right at the small church, passing some houses built around a courtyard.

4 Agriculture

Notice the red soil in this area. Its high fertility supports the region's extensive potato crop. In the distance the visitor may hear the motor of the water pumps; many of these are driven by steel windmills, one of which is visible in the distance from the path.

Walk across the scrubland. There is a small beach to the left, and after about 200m (220yds) the path reaches the Pierre Anne Beach Hotel. Follow the track at its far end, skirting the swimming pool, and head towards the sea.

The track now enters a ditch. Cross this and skirt round a bamboo grove, keeping close to the sea. Emerge on to a beach (this is a half-hour walk from the harbour).

Take the track which rises gently on to the headland.

5 Headland

From here there are wonderful views: to the east lies Cape Gkreko, to the west, a stretch of rocky coast, and

The monastery of Agia Napa

in the distance, the far promontory of Nissi Beach. The headland has the typical spiky rocks of the area.

From the headland walk on the track which bears right and leads suddenly into a sandy cove, known as Sandy Bay. Walkers can return the way they came or walk along the main road, Leoforos Nissi. There is a footpath on the right-hand side of the road.

6 Leoforos Nissi

The route passes hotels and apartments with some pockets of agricultural land with windmills. The road soon acquires all the tourist trappings of shops and cafés.

After 0.5km (¹/₃ mile) Leoforos Archiepiskopou Makariou III is reached. Turn right to regain the harbour area.

Greek weddings

Getting married remains the assumed destiny of most Cypriot girls. Just over a decade or two ago, young women were chaperoned and casual acquaintance with men was unacceptable, and Greek-Cypriot weddings still carry their own unique character and expectations.

Couples are often quite young when they marry. An accepted tradition was that the groom's family provided a means of income for the couple, usually a job or a business, while the bride's family would provide a dowry or a house for them to live in.

In Cyprus, families usually own plots of land inherited from their parents, and the birth of a daughter has traditionally signalled a time to start thinking about building a house on a plot for when she marries. Times have changed though and now, with the pressures of modern-day life, both families tend to help the couple towards purchasing a home and starting their future together.

The government in Cyprus legally accepts civil weddings, but the majority of Greek Cypriots still marry in the ornate splendour of a Greek Orthodox church, where a ceremony is performed by one or more priests. It is a joyous and deeply religious occasion, and yet if you are lucky enough to be invited to one you may be quite startled by the antics of the congregation. It is not uncommon to see children playing and adult guests on their mobile phones while the service is in progress.

There are two very distinct types of wedding. In town, people are invited through advertisements in the newspaper, which usually means a

Everyone in the village actively participates in a wedding, which is flamboyant in its ceremonies, dress and music

Village weddings often include a ceremonial 'last shave' by the groom's friends

large crowd. Weddings are generally held on a Sunday and the reception held in a large hotel or restaurant. The guests queue up to shake hands with the couple and their parents, offer an envelope containing money and receive a piece of sweet cake or some sugared almonds. Guests are then invited to feast. As guest numbers can reach a couple of thousand, you are not expected to stay after you have eaten but leave to make space at your table so more guests can sit and eat.

In the villages the wedding is a more riotous affair. Traditions vary but often include a ceremonial shaving of the groom and the ritual dance around the mattress of the couple. At other times a baby will be rolled across the mattress to promote fertility in the newly weds.

The whole village is invited to the wedding, which takes place in the street. Guests are also expected to greet the couple and their parents, and offer a gift of money. Long wooden tables are set up and guests are served a substantial meal of *kleftiko*: lamb slow-roasted with herbs in a traditional oven. The singing and dancing then goes on all night.

The south

With the exception of the elevated village of Pano Lefkara, only the coastal strip is covered in this section. Governor's Beach forms the eastern extremity and Pissouri Beach the western. All along there is a backcloth of hills, 3–4km (2–2½ miles) inland. The foothills of the Troodos Mountains start their steady ascent to the highest ridges of the massif.

To the east of Lemesos (Limassol) the coast is splendid, with the highlight being Governor's Beach, between Larnaka and Lemesos, a fine beach in a dramatic chalky landscape. To the west the scenery is even better, starting with the cliff-top site of Kourion, and the beaches of Avdimou (Evdhimou) and Pissouri, by Cape Aspron (White Cape).

To the south of Lemesos is the rather unappealing Akrotiri Peninsula, where Lady's Mile Beach extends to Cape Gata and its colonies of falcons. This is British Sovereign Base territory, one of two on the island, with a large salt lake.

In summer, it turns into an expanse of grey mudflats, which give off the distinctive smell of salt. The airstrip by the lake thunders to the sound of Royal Air Force jets which shatter the peace of the nearby Agios Nikolaos Ton Gaten Convent. At the northern edge of the peninsula are the Fasouri (Phasouri) plantations, a great abundance of citrus groves traversed by straight tree-covered avenues.

The old road west to Pafos (not the motorway) passes through Episkopi Garrison, where the green amphitheatre of the playing fields, with its housing estates on the hills, has a hint of England about it, made complete should a game of cricket be under way.

Lemesos (Limassol), the second-largest town in Cyprus, is the centre of everything for the area. It is large, with a variety of industries and a flourishing commercial life. The port is extensive and busy, with ships from all over the world. Lemesos is also the centre of Cyprus's wine industry, complete with four big producers. Cyprus's Keo beer is also brewed here. Known as an entertainment centre, Lemesos is famous for its carnivals and festivals.

The city is not confined to commerce and industry. For many years it welcomed tourists, and there are a huge number of hotels here.

The famous ruins of Amathous to the east once stood in splendid isolation, but today they are joined to Lemesos by 10km (6 miles) of hotels along a shore of man-made beaches.

LEMESOS (LIMASSOL)
Amathous

Amathous was one of the ancient city kingdoms of Cyprus and the remains on this site date back to 1000 BC. Amathous prospered because of its port, which allowed it to export copper and timber. This prosperity was brought to an end by a combination of earthquakes and Arab raids. By 1191, when Richard the Lionheart landed here, it had been completely abandoned and the tombs plundered.

The best sites to explore are Acropolis Hill and the *agora* (marketplace). On the hill, by the remains of a stone jar, are the ruins of the Temple of Apollo.

At the foot of the hill, signposted from the road, is a fenced site containing the pillars of the Roman/Byzantine *agora*. This was destroyed in an earthquake in the 4th century, but a good impression can still be gained.

In the grounds of the Amathous Beach Hotel is an underground tomb, part of the western necropolis. There are many other tombs on the site. Archaeologists are currently uncovering the remains of the ancient harbour.
8km (5 miles) east of Lemesos city centre, on the old coast road. Open: Apr–May & Sept–Oct daily 8am–6pm; Jun–Aug daily 8am–7.30pm; Nov–Mar daily 8am–5pm. Admission charge.

Carob Museum

This fascinating museum traces the history and production processes of the carob. It is housed in a renovated, high-tech building used for processing carobs in the 1990s.
Voisilissis, behind castle. Tel: 25 762 828. Open: daily 10am–8pm.

Folk Art Museum

This is a collection of Cypriot folk art from the 19th and 20th centuries. Displays include national costumes, tapestry and embroidery.
Agiou Andreou 253. Tel: 25 362 303. Open: Jun–Sept Mon–Wed & Fri 8.30am–1.30pm & 4–6.30pm, Thur 8.30am–1.30pm; Oct–May Mon–Wed & Fri 8.30am–1.30pm & 3–5.30pm, Thur 8.30am–1.30pm. Closed: Sat & Sun. Admission charge.

Ancient stone artefacts at Lemesos Castle

Lemesos (Limassol) (*see pp68–9 for walk route*)

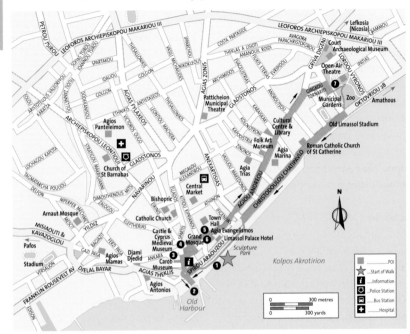

Lemesos Castle and Cyprus Medieval Museum

The present castle is 600 years old, although it was built on the site of an earlier fort. Its chapel, no longer in existence, is believed to have been used for the marriage of Richard the Lionheart and Berengaria, who made an unscheduled stop here on their way to the Third Crusade. The castle was further fortified by the Ottoman Turks and now houses an excellent medieval museum. On the ground floor, coats of arms, tombstones and wall paintings are displayed.

Upstairs are some splendid weapons and two complete suits of armour, together with some superb medieval pottery, jewellery and stone gargoyles.

The spiral staircase leads up to the battlements, from where there are extensive views out across the city.

Downstairs in the basement are photographs of all the Byzantine churches across the island, with copies of tombstones found in the Cathedral of Santa Sophia in Lefkosia (Nicosia).
*Eirinis, just north of the old harbour.
Tel: 25 305 419.
Open: Tue–Sat 9am–5pm, Sun
10am–1pm. Closed: Mon.
Admission charge.*

Lemesos District Archaeological Museum

Room 1 has axe heads and tools from the Neolithic period. Room 2 contains pottery and jewellery, while Room 3 has particularly impressive statues of the Egyptian god Bes and a headless statue of Zeus, both found at Amathous.

North of the Municipal Gardens at the junction of Kannigkos and Vyronos. Tel: 25 305 157. Open: Tue, Wed & Fri 8am–3pm, Thur 8am–5pm, Sat 9am–3pm. Closed: Mon & Sun. Admission charge.

Zoo and Municipal Gardens

The gardens are a pleasant, well-watered spot, with benches aligned along wide pathways. They provide a welcome relief from the bustle outside. One corner holds a small zoo. In September, the gardens host the annual wine festival (*see p19*), where stalls are set up by the various wine companies.

RICHARD THE LIONHEART

It was at Lemesos that Richard the Lionheart landed in 1191. He was on the Third Crusade but came ashore to rescue his fiancée, Berengaria, whose ship had been wrecked off the Lemesos coast during a storm.

Following a disagreement with the island's ruler, Isaac Comnenos, Richard then routed him in battle. During this unscheduled stop, he married his betrothed, Berengaria, crowning her Queen of England.

It seems Lionheart was unsure what to do with the conquered island, which had more or less fallen into his lap. Being short of money for his Crusades, he sold it to the Knights Templar and made a great haul of booty. They found it too troublesome and gave it back to him at some financial loss.

Eventually the English king passed it on to a certain Norman knight, Guy de Lusignan, and the durable Lusignan dynasty of Cyprus was created.

Oktovriou 28. Open: gardens, daylight hours; zoo, daily 9am–6.30pm. Admission charge only for zoo.

The south

The zoo gardens at Lemesos

Walk: Lemesos

Lemesos (Limassol) is one of the principal industrial and commercial centres of the island. This walk explores the main sites of interest and shopping districts of the town.

See the map on p66 for the route.

Allow 1 hour, longer if you visit the castle.

Start from the car park on the seafront, almost opposite the Sculpture Park.

1 Seafront

The attractive seafront is wide and palm-lined with a narrow sand beach in parts. Offshore there is always a long queue of ships waiting to enter the port at the far west of the city. *Initially, take the road nearest the sea (with the sea on your left), at the western end of the Sculpture Park. Then, after 5 minutes' walking, move inland to join the main road and pass several shops selling souvenirs, pottery and copper goods. Continue to a roundabout, and turn left towards the old harbour.*

2 Harbour

This is the old harbour, now serving only pleasure and fishing boats. The new port is several kilometres to the west. In the early morning, fishermen land their catch here and set up their stalls to sell it.

Turn right at the roundabout to reach the castle on the left-hand side of the road.

3 Lemesos Castle and Cyprus Medieval Museum

Lying in pleasant grounds, the current building was constructed in the 14th century. It is said that Richard the Lionheart married Berengaria in the castle chapel (no longer visible). The castle now houses a fine medieval museum with three levels. In the dungeon are artefacts from Byzantine churches; on the ground floor is a wide range of tombstones and wall paintings; and upstairs are some very impressive suits of armour.

It is also possible to climb right up to the battlements and look out over the city.

On leaving the castle, take the first road to the right, and 100m (110yds) away is the Grand Mosque of Lemesos.

Elegant wall carvings at Agia Evangelismos

4 Grand Mosque

This mosque is still in use, and visitors may enter if they are modestly dressed.

Leave the mosque, and enter an arched shopping arcade. Pass through here and turn right into Agiou Andreou.

5 Agiou Andreou

This is one of the main shopping streets in Lemesos, with many shops selling lace and leather goods. Souvenir shops rub shoulders with chic boutiques. This is Cyprus's best shopping without a doubt.

After about 200m (220yds) the road fans out, and ahead is a large church, Agia Evanegelismos.

6 Agia Evangelismos

This is a large modern church decorated in an ornate style.

Continue ahead on Agiou Andreou until a pedestrianised area is reached, and then turn right down Ifigeneias.

A shop of the Cyprus Handicraft Service is on the right, just before the street reaches the seafront. Continue along Agiou Andreou. Agia Trias Church is off a side street to the left, and the Folk Art Museum (see p65) is at the junction with Kapodistria St. Very soon, Tanagrea Ceramics, opposite Androutsou, is seen on the right. Proceed a little further before turning right along Giagkou Tornariti to the Municipal Gardens.

7 Municipal Gardens

The Lemesos Wine Festival is held here in the first two weeks of September when there are many stalls and great revelry. At other times of the year it is a quiet place, well watered and remarkably green. There is a small zoo at the eastern end of the gardens.

Turn down to the seafront, and return to the starting point passing the Roman Catholic Church of St Catherine.

Governor's Beach is protected by cliffs behind

Agiou Nikolaou (Monastery)

This monastery was founded in AD 325 and rebuilt in the 13th century. The cat population of Cyprus was introduced here to keep down the snakes. The monastery is often closed for siesta between noon and 3pm.

13km (8 miles) south of Lemesos in the British Sovereign Base of Akrotiri. The main gate to the base closes at 4pm.

Avdimou (Evdhimou) Beach

This is an excellent and relatively unspoilt beach, its position within the boundary of the British Sovereign Base of Episkopi keeping holiday development at bay. There is a long stretch of sand with good swimming from the jetty, although the water can get deep very quickly.

3km (2 miles) off the Pafos Rd, opposite turning to Avdimou village.

Choirokoitia (Khirokitia)

Discovered in 1934, this Neolithic site is the second-earliest known settlement on the island and dates back to at least 6800 BC. Only Kastros, on the Karpaz Peninsula, predates it.

It is easy to see why the site was chosen by early settlers. It has a good defensive position on fertile land, with a permanent water supply. The large number of agricultural implements found here suggests that it was a settled farming community, although they also hunted wild animals.

Further evidence of the residents' way of life comes from their graves, which were dug in the floor of the houses. In one house as many as twenty-six burials were found in eight superimposed floors. The bodies were surrounded by gifts. A large stone was placed on the chests of the dead, perhaps to prevent them coming back to haunt the living. The sheer number of graves indicates how densely populated the site must have been.

While the place is extremely significant in archaeological terms, the casual visitor may find it hard to discern the extent of the ruins. The main points of interest lie on either side of what was once the main street. Five levels of building from different periods have been discovered and it seems that when one house collapsed, another was simply built on top of it.

In the first area the visitor will see the ruins of the distinctive beehive-shaped houses for which the site is famous. These were made of stones from the river, with mud bricks laid on top. Some of the houses had several storeys. The most easily discernible dwelling is House A, near the entrance, at almost 9m (30ft) across.

In the second group of ruins there are the remains of pillars which once supported a roof. Some of the most interesting graves were found in this area, including one of a middle-aged woman, buried with her jewellery. In some cases, the thickness of the house walls is up to 3m (10ft).

The best view of the site is gained from the far end, at the top of the hill (and many stairs), where the visitor can acquire a perspective of the whole area.

The site is off junction 14 on the Lefkosia–Lemesos motorway. Tel: 24 322 710. Open: Apr–May & Sept–Oct daily 8am–6pm; Jun–Aug daily 8am–7.30pm; Nov–Mar daily 8am–5pm. Admission charge.

Governor's Beach

Lying at the bottom of low white cliffs, the dark-coloured sand can get unbearably hot. The small beach is often extremely busy at weekends. *29km (18 miles) east of Lemesos.*

Kolossi Castle

A fort was first built on this site by the Knights Hospitaller and soon became their headquarters. The surrounding area is very fertile and the Knights made full use of their land to make the Order the richest on the island.

After attacks by the Genoese and Mamelukes, the castle had to be rebuilt and these are the buildings we see today.

Visitors enter across the drawbridge into a sort of reception hall where a

Visitors will encounter a small drawbridge at the entrance to Kolossi Castle

mural of the Crucifixion resides. The rooms all have high vaulted ceilings and those on the upper floors are extremely light and airy with grand fireplaces. In contrast, the rooms in the basement are very dark.

There are some interesting out-buildings in the gardens.

14km (9 miles) west of Lemesos. Tel: 25 934 907. Open: Apr–May daily 8am–6pm; Jun–Aug daily 8am–7.30pm; Sept–Oct daily 8am–6pm; Nov–Mar daily 8am–5pm. Admission charge.

Kourion (Curium)

After Salamis, this is the most impressive archaeological site on the island. It is wonderfully situated on the cliffs above the Mediterranean.

The site has been inhabited since the Neolithic period, and was colonised in turn by the Mycenaeans, Dorians and Achaeans. By 673 BC, Kourion had become one of several city-states on the island. The main settlement had moved to the present location on the cliff top from the original site near Episkopi village, where some of the oldest tombs have been found. At the same time, the **Sanctuary of Apollo Hylates** was built west of the main city (*see p74*).

Kourion played a central role in the battle against the Persians. After fighting on the Greek side for much of the war the city defected to the Persians at a crucial point, a decision which was paramount in bringing Persian control to the whole island.

Kourion

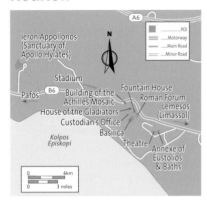

The Roman period was one of great prosperity for the city but it was followed by a devastating earthquake in the 4th century. The city was further damaged by Arab raids in the 7th century, leading to the abandonment of the cliff-top site.

Today, however, the ruins provide a compelling glimpse of the past. The entrance to the site is to the east, at the bottom of the long hill, past tiny Agios Ermogenis Monastery. Here is found the **amphitheatre**, one of the most photographed sites on the island. What the visitor sees today is not the original auditorium but a reconstruction based on the evidence revealed by excavation.

It seems the original theatre was built in the 2nd century but a hundred years later was extended to allow for displays of combat with animals; the lower row of seats was removed to keep the spectators at a safe distance. The theatre was finally abandoned in the 4th century.

Today, there is a corridor around the back of the amphitheatre, with stone paths leading to the seating area. Up to 3,500 people can be seated here and the theatre is still used for productions. The tourist office has programme details.

Further east, but higher up the hill, is the covered **Annexe of Eustolios**. Visitors walk through on raised gangways. Constructed in about the 5th century, it features very well-preserved mosaics.

Steps lead up to the **baths**, where more mosaics are to be found. These include a depiction of a partridge and a bust of Ktisis, a female representation of the Creation. Off the central room were the cold baths, the medium-heated room and the hot room. Some of the remains of the heating system are also visible.

On the high ground at the other end of the site is the **basilica**, built in the 5th century. It was a very grand

building with its roof supported by 12 columns. The bases of some of these can still be made out in places. The whole building was exceptionally large, 70m by 40m (230ft by 130ft). Some fragments of original mosaic are still visible.

A little further on is the **House of the Gladiators**, containing a mosaic of two gladiators fighting. Also visible from here is the aqueduct which used to supply the city's water.

Finally, and now some 500m (¹⁄₃ mile) from the theatre, one comes upon the **Building of the Achilles Mosaic**. It was clearly a grand structure which was probably used to receive important visitors. The mosaic shows Achilles dressed as a woman, but despite his disguise he is recognised by Odysseus. A depiction of Ganymede and the eagle can be seen in a smaller room.

A short distance away on the inland side of the road to Pafos are the remains of the **stadium**. It was built in the 2nd century AD and remained in use until about AD 400. Its U shape, three entrances and some of its seven-tier seating can still be made out. In its day, 6,000 people could be accommodated here.

The Kourion amphitheatre is still used for open-air productions

The main site is 19km (12 miles) from Lemesos, off the Pafos Rd. The stadium lies unfenced, 800m (¹⁄₂ mile) to the west of the main site. Tel: 25 934 250. Open: Apr–May & Sept–Oct daily 8am–6pm; Jun–Aug daily 8am–7.30pm; Nov–Mar daily 8am–5pm. Admission charge.

Ieron Appollonos
(Sanctuary of Apollo Hylates)
This is another important archaeological site. In ancient times it was part of the city of Kourion and was one of the most important destinations of pilgrimage on the island. There is evidence that worship of Apollo started here as early as the 8th century BC, although the existing buildings date from AD 100.

Visitors enter on a marked track and will see the remains of the dormitories in front of them. Skirting round to the left is the display hall, the steps of which can still be made out. Adjoining this is the votive pit, where the priests put unwanted religious offerings. From here, a short way down the track, is the restored area of the temple itself, which was very small; the rituals must presumably have taken place outside.

A roof and fence protect the ruins of the Priest's House, which contains mosaics and pottery. At the end of

Ieron Appollonos is an ancient site of pilgrimage and worship

the circuit are the remains of the *palaestra*, where sporting displays took place. The big, stone water jar in the corner was used by the athletes. There are also the remains of some baths, just behind the *palaestra*. As at Kourion, there was a sequence of rooms running from the cold room to the hot room and back again.
3km (2 miles) northwest of Kourion. Open: Apr–May & Sept–Oct daily 8am–6pm; Jun–Aug daily 8am–7.30pm; Nov–Mar daily 8am–5pm. Admission charge.

Kourion Museum
The museum is in an old house in the village of Episkopi. The collection kept here was started by an American archaeologist in 1937.

On display are terracotta chariots, lamps, figurines and limestone heads, plus a multitude of ancient artefacts from the surrounding area.
At village centre, by the church. Tel: 25 932 453. Open: Mon–Wed & Fri 9am–2.30pm, Thur 9am–2.30pm & 3–5pm. Closed: Sat & Sun. Admission charge.

Lady's Mile Beach
Lady's Mile Beach is an extremely long and popular stretch of sand. The further away from Lemesos, the better the shore and the better the road. The area is not always peaceful, with military jets taking off from the RAF base behind.
Akrotiri Peninsula, 8km (5 miles) southwest of Lemesos.

Lefkara

Lefkara lies in the mountains, split into two halves: Pano (Upper) Lefkara and Kato (Lower) Lefkara. The village has become a very popular tourist destination and features in many organised tours.

Its main claim to fame comes from its lacemaking tradition. Lefkara became renowned for lace in the Venetian period – it appears the Venetian nobility used the village as a summer resort and brought their seamstresses with them. The art then caught on with the locals, and they began to produce their own distinctive product, Lefkaritika lace. Leonardo da Vinci is said to have been so impressed that he ordered a substantial quantity to decorate Milan Cathedral.

It was not until the late 19th century, however, that the village's reputation was firmly established. A forceful businesswoman, Theofyla Antoni, set up a lacemaking school and travelled the Mediterranean exporting her product. These days, equally formidable women try to cajole tourists into their lace shops.

The upper village is the main tourist centre, with shops all along its length. The streets form a maze and those driving through the village will need to take care. The best place to park is at the far side of the village.

In the upper village, the church has some impressive 18th-century icons and a silver cross, 500 years older still.

A lacemaker's house at Lefkara

There is a small museum of lace-making and embroidery in a restored house, signed from the main street.

The lower village boasts cafés, tavernas and more lace shops. It is very peaceful, with distinctive blue-painted houses and restful views of the surrounding hills.

9km (5¹/₂ miles) off junction 13 on the Lefkosia–Lemesos motorway.
Museum. Tel: 24 342 326. Open: Mon–Thur 9.30am–4pm, Fri & Sat 10am–4pm. Closed: Sun. Admission charge.

Pissouri

This is a tempting stretch of sand surrounded by white cliffs and a safe sea, ideal for swimming. There are some hotels, but the village of narrow streets is on a cliff top, 3km (2 miles) away.
34km (21 miles) west of Lemesos.

The west

Western Cyprus consists of a region of high ground, an attractive coastal strip and some good beaches. The area starts by the fabled rocks of Petra tou Romiou (Rock of Romios), and includes the town of Pafos and the western seaboard. Also included is the majestic semicircle of Chrysochou Bay to Akra Pomou (Pomos Point) and beyond to Kato Pyrgos. This is literally the end of the Green Line; the UN division that starts in Gazimağusa in the east, and traverses the island, ends here.

The isolated Turkish village of Erenköy (Kokkina in Greek) cannot be entered and travellers are obliged to detour up the mountain before regaining the coast. The tiny island of Limnitis with its ruined Neolithic settlement can be seen just offshore.

Fine beaches exist to the east of Pomos Point. It is here that the western Troodos Mountains run down close to the sea. From the coast road all routes, good sealed roads, lead inland up the valleys. The village of most significance in Chrysochou Bay is Polis and it is growing in popularity. However, it is further west, at the once-tiny fishing harbour of Latchi, that holiday development has taken place.

Western Cyprus is greener than the rest of the island. A striking feature of the area around Pafos is the banana plantations. Pafos, a busy tourist town, is a good base for exploring this part of the island, although each season sees it busier than before. Down by the sea the town has expanded rapidly, some parts nudging against the archaeological wonders of the area.

The old part of the town, Kitma, sits on a plateau away from the sea. It is a place of government buildings, typical old shops that have changed little over the years, and museums. The coastal strip below the Kitma Plateau is called Kato Pafos. This distinction has been made to avoid confusion with Palaepaphos to the east. Its main attraction is the harbour with its medieval fort, cafés and tavernas.

PAFOS
History
Pafos (Paphos) was founded in about 300 BC and rapidly became an important administrative and commercial centre. The Romans found it to their liking and constructed many buildings by the sea. However, as with all the ancient cities of Cyprus, Pafos was twice devastated by earthquakes in the 4th century. The town's gradual decline was arrested when the British took over in 1878.

Pafos (Paphos) (*see pp82–3 for walk route*)

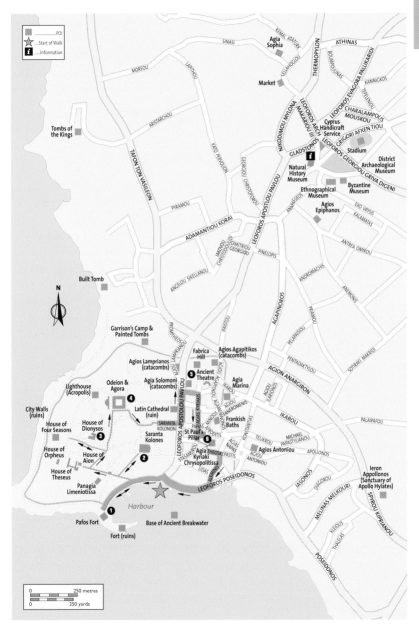

POI
Start of Walk
i Information

Agia Sophia
SINASI
KEMAL ATATURK
BOLIMPOULINAS
THERMOPYLON
ATHINAS
MOREOU
LAPTHIOU
Market
FELLAHOGLOU
LEOFOROS EVAGORA PALIKARIDI
KANNIKKOS
TERELENGU
NIKODIMOU MYLONA
LEOFOROS ARCH
MAKARIOU III
LEOFOROS GRIGORI AFXEN TIOU
LEOFOROS CHARALAMPOUS MOUSKOU
Cyprus Handicraft Service
ARISTARCHOU
GLADSTONOS
Stadium
LEOFOROS GEORGIOU GRIVA DIGENI
District Archaeological Museum
Tombs of the Kings
TAFON TON VASILEON
KATO PERVOLION
GEORGIOU CHRISTODOU
Natural History Museum
LEOFOROS APOSTOLOU PAVLOU
Ethnographical Museum
Byzantine Museum
EXO VRYSIS
PYRAMOU
Agios Epiphanos
KALAMATAS
ADAMANTIOU KORAI
IAKONOU CHRISTODOU
DIMITRIOU GEORGIOU
PINELOPIS
ANTREA OMIROU
ANGELOU SKELLANOU
ANDROMACHIS
ANIMONIS
Built Tomb
PRIANOU
N
AGAPINOROS
PELARGOU
PENTADAKTYLOU
SOTIRAI MAKRIDI
Garrison's Camp & Painted Tombs
PROMITHEOS
LAPRIANOU
Fabrica Hill
Agios Agapitikos (catacombs)
AGION ANARGIRON
Agios Lamprianos (catacombs)
⑤
Ancient Theatre
Agia Marina
Agia Solomoni (catacombs)
AGIOU ILARIONOS
IKAROU
PALAIPAFOU
Lighthouse (Acropolis)
Odeion & Agora
④
Latin Cathedral (ruin)
AGIAS KYRIAKIS
PAFIAS APROTITIS
AGION MAVROMENIS
FANEROMENIS
City Walls (ruins)
House of Four Seasons
House of Dionysos
③
SARANTA KOLONON
Saranta Kolones
St Paul's Pillar
⑥
Frankish Baths
KONSTANTINOU
TEUKROU
MICHAEL PAPASTYLIANOU
APOLLONOS
House of Orpheus
House of Aion
②
Agia Kyriaki Chrysopolitissa
AGIAS THEOSKEPASTIS
AGIOU ANTONIOU
NAPAS
Agios Antoniou
Ieron Appollonos (Sanctuary of Apollo Hylates)
House of Theseus
Panagia Limeniotissa
LIDAS
ALMINIOU
LEOFOROS POSEIDONOS
IASONOS
DIAGOROU
MELINAS MELKOURI
SPYROU KIPRIANOU
①
Harbour
Pafos Fort
Base of Ancient Breakwater
KLEOUS
THALLEAS
Fort (ruins)
POSEIDONOS

0 ____ 250 metres
0 ____ 250 yards

Agia Kyriaki Chrysopolitissa and St Paul's Pillar

The small church of Agia Kyriaki Chrysopolitissa was built in the 12th century and is still used for Catholic Mass. The site is a place of reverence for Christians, containing the pillar at which St Paul was allegedly flogged when he came to the island to convert the governor to Christianity. He failed, and was given 39 lashes for his pains. However, it seems that the governor later relented and he subsequently became a Christian.

The pillar stands at the far end of the site, one of several in an extensive area which is thought to have been the Roman forum.

Stasandrou, east of Leoforos Apostolou Pavlou. Open: normally daily during daylight hours. Free admission.

Agia Solomoni and Agios Lamprianos catacombs

These catacombs are very old, but it was not until the Byzantine period that Agia Solomoni was first used as a Christian church. Remnants of religious paintings cover the walls, badly damaged by water and by graffiti. The tree outside is bedecked with pieces of clothing which are left here in the hope that they will cure the afflicted part on which they have been rubbed.

Agios Lamprianos has a similar history but has not been so extensively excavated.
Leoforos Apostolou Pavlou, northern end of Kato Pafos. Open: normally daily. Free admission.

Byzantine Castle

The castle is also known as Saranta Kolones (40 columns) after the columns found on the site. Many of these, in grey granite, are still visible.

The castle was probably built in the 7th century to safeguard the town from attack by Arab raiders. After the earthquake of 1222, it was abandoned. It originally contained a square keep with a 3m- (10ft-) thick outer wall, fronted by a moat. There were towers at each corner, and some can still be made out.

The castle is fun to explore because there are still spiral staircases to descend and the remnants of dungeons and towers visible. Take care on the unguarded high walls.
Within Pafos Archaeological Site, by the harbour. Open: Apr–May & Sept–Oct daily 8am–6pm; Jun–Aug daily 8am–7.30pm; Nov–Mar daily 8am–5pm. Admission charge for Archaeological Site.

Byzantine Museum

This is a small museum in the upper town. It houses mainly religious items, including Byzantine icons from the 12th to 18th centuries and woodcarvings. Close by are the arches of the Bishopric, surrounding a pleasant courtyard.
Pafos Bishopric, Andreas Ioannou 5, old town. Tel: 26 931 393. Open: summer Mon–Fri 9am–4pm; winter Mon–Fri 9am–3pm; Sat 9am–1pm. Closed: Sun. Admission charge.

District Archaeological Museum

This museum houses a fascinating array of finds from local excavations. Room 1 contains steatite idols and a skeleton from Empa. Room 2 has pottery from the classical Greek period, jewellery, glassware and lamps, and a collection of coins. Room 3 includes several sarcophagi and clay hot-water bottles shaped to fit different parts of the body. Rooms 4 and 5 display numerous statues, jars and pottery from the Roman and medieval periods. Other statues occupy the garden.

Leoforos Georgiou Griva Digeni 43. Tel: 26 306 215. Open: Mon, Wed & Fri 8am–3pm, Thur 8am–5pm, Sat 9am–3pm. Closed: Tue & Sun. Admission charge.

Ethnographical Museum

This is the private collection of George Eliades, who enthusiastically amassed an extensive range of artefacts from Cyprus's past. The exhibits include axe heads, amphorae, coins and kitchen utensils. There is also a reconstructed bridal chamber, with traditional costumes and furniture. In the garden are two tombs from the 3rd century BC.

Exo Vrisis 1, near the Bishopric. Tel: 26 932 010. Open: Mon–Fri 10am–5.30pm, Sat 10am–5pm. Closed: Sun. Admission charge.

Mosaics of Pafos

The mosaics are in four main houses: House of Dionysos, House of Theseus, House of Orpheus and House of

The Byzantine castle Saranta Kolones overlooking Pafos harbour

A mosaic at the House of Dionysos

showing five scenes. At the top left is Leda and the swan (Zeus is disguised as the swan). In the top right corner is a picture of baby nymphs with the baby Dionysos. The middle picture shows sea nymphs in a beauty contest, being judged by Aion. In the bottom row Dionysos appears again in a triumphal procession, and the final picture shows Apollo (god of music) punishing the loser of a musical duel.

The **House of Orpheus** contains, among others, a very impressive depiction of Orpheus surrounded by animals who are listening to his music. The **House of Theseus** is found in two sheds at the far side of the site. The mosaics here are less well preserved. The best are in the south wing, where Theseus himself can be seen. A fifth house – the **Four Seasons** – discovered in 1992 shows the Gods of the Four Seasons hunting. *Within Pafos Archaeological Site, by the harbour. Open: Apr–May & Sept–Oct daily 8am–6pm; Jun–Aug daily 8am–7.30pm; Nov–Mar daily 8am–5pm. Admission charge for Archaeological Site.*

Aion, all of which date from around the 3rd century AD.

The **House of Dionysos** is the largest and has the most impressive mosaics. In the far corner is a mosaic depicting Ganymede and the eagle. The inner set of mosaics shows some animated hunting scenes. The highlight of the house is a series of scenes relating to Dionysos, including what is claimed to be the first depiction of a hangover in history.

A short distance away is the **House of Aion**, the smallest house, discovered in 1983. It contains one large mosaic

Odeion

This is a small restored theatre with 12 rows of seats visible. It was built in the 2nd century but badly damaged in an earthquake, being abandoned in the 7th century.

Also on the site, although less easily discernible, are the remains of the acropolis and of the *agora*

(marketplace). The foundations and stumps of the columns of the latter are still visible and it was probably built at the same time as the theatre.
Within Pafos Archaeological Site, by the harbour. Open: Apr–May & Sept–Oct daily 8am–6pm; Jun–Aug daily 8am–7.30pm; Nov–Mar daily 8am–5pm. Admission charge for Archaeological Site.

Pafos Fort

The fort, on the harbour wall, was built by the Lusignans to defend the town against seaborne attack. However, the Ottoman Turks still managed to capture Pafos with little difficulty, then reused the fort as a prison.

The building has recently been undergoing restoration. Visitors enter across a drawbridge and can climb on to the battlements or explore the dungeons.
Western end of the harbour. Open: Apr–May & Sept–Oct daily 8am–6pm; Jun–Aug daily 8am–7.30pm; Nov–Mar daily 8am–5pm. Admission charge.

Tombs of the Kings

Although no royalty was buried here, it seems that the tombs were deemed so majestic that they were given this royal appellation.

There are approximately 100 tombs on the site, which lies on the headland, with good views of the coast below. Visitors should take care on the top of the tombs, which date from about the 3rd century BC. These were cut out of the rock and built around a courtyard with Doric columns. They are numbered, the most impressive lying towards the middle of the site. It is possible to climb down the steps and enter most of the tombs, some of which are spectacular.
Take the road signed Coral Bay from Pafos, and after 1.5km (1 mile) the entrance is to the left. Tel: 26 306 217. Open: Apr–May & Sept–Oct daily 8am–6pm; Jun–Aug daily 8am–7.30pm; Nov–Mar daily 8am–5pm. Admission charge.

The picturesque Pafos Fort looks out over the harbour

Walk: Pafos

The walk explores the lower town of Pafos, which contains some of the most impressive archaeological sites on the island.

See the map on p77 for the route.

Allow 1 hour for the walk, longer if the sights are to be thoroughly explored.

Start at the junction of Leoforos Apostolou Pavlou and Leoforos Poseidonos, right by the seafront. Follow the line of the promenade to the harbour.

1 Harbour and Pafos Fort

The harbour is a pleasant place, still used by the local fishermen. There were originally two forts guarding the entrance. The older one, out on the breakwater, now consists of only two lumps of rock. The other was built by the Lusignans to defend the town against pirate raiders. The dungeons and battlements are the main points of interest.

Return along the harbourside to the entrance of Pafos Archaeological Site, on the left after the last of the restaurants.

The first section of the walk is through the site and its antiquities. The entry fee gives access to the famous mosaics (see pp79–80), Odeion (see pp80–81), Saranta Kolones or Byzantine Castle (see p78) and lesser-known ruins.

2 Byzantine Castle

It is better to visit this first as it would be quite a detour later. It is a fascinating place to scramble around, with many dungeons and arches. A large number of the original 40 grey stone columns can be seen lying about the site.

Return to the site entrance and follow the path up the hill to the mosaics.

3 Mosaics

This is a huge complex on the hill with the most spectacular mosaics displayed in covered sheds. The House of Dionysos contains the most extensive range, but there are four other houses on the site – those of Aion, Orpheus, Theseus and the Four Seasons – all worth exploring. Excavations are still being conducted; some areas may be closed.

Return to the main path and turn left up the slope to the Odeion and lighthouse.

4 Odeion

The most distinctive ruin is that of the Roman Odeion Theatre, which has been partially restored. In front of the Odeion was the *agora,* or marketplace, but only a few columns remain.

This high vantage point has excellent views across the site and Kato Pafos. *From here the route is generally east, but as the entire site is fenced it is essential to follow the makeshift sign for Leoforos Apostolou Pavlou to find the exit. Turn left at the avenue and in about 250m (275yds), on the right-hand side, are the catacombs of Agia Solomoni.*

5 Agia Solomoni

The catacombs are easily recognisable from the tree outside, which has been bedecked with handkerchiefs tied by visitors, who hope they will be cured of their maladies. The catacombs are still in use as a church and have an altar. *Go east along the road at the side of the catacombs for 100m (110yds) and*

turn right down Agias Kyriakis. In 300m (330yds) the junction with Stilis Agiou Pavlou is reached, with the partially fenced-off site of St Paul's Pillar close by.

6 St Paul's Pillar

This site, some of which is still being excavated, has the interesting church of Agia Kyriaki Chrysopolitissa in one corner, where Mass is still held. Many columns punctuate the area, but it is a small pillar marked by a plaque, only visible through a fence, that most people come to see. This is where St Paul is alleged to have been given 39 lashes on the orders of the Roman governor, who objected to his preaching Christianity.
Wander south to the seafront through the side streets and then turn right along the promenade and back to the harbour.

Walk: Pafos

Agia Kyriaki Chrysopolitissa Church with the remains of a much larger cathedral in its grounds

Walk: Aspros Gorge

The walk is for fine weather only, and not for those who prefer a clear track; paths in these parts come and go. Although much of the route is along the lip of the ravine, with common sense it is not dangerous. Nevertheless, no attempt should be made to enter the gorge except where described.

Allow 2½ hours for this 7km (4-mile) walk and take plenty of liquids in hot weather.

Start at the north side of the gorge, and follow the winding track about 600m (660yds) up the hill to some fencing. In another 100m (110yds) bear right at a junction, by the E4 marker posts. In some 300m (330yds) turn right

at a T-junction. A metal shed is soon reached and here there is a short diversion, off right, to an excellent viewing platform. Continue on the main route and descend to two bridges crossing the gorge.

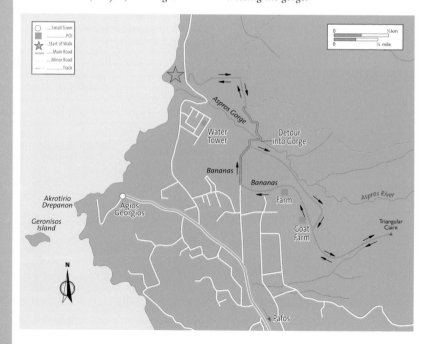

Gorge bed

Climb out of the ravine on the southern side. Carry on forward until you reach a cairn, marked 1, by a walled track.

Through the trees

The route forward from the cairn is not obvious. It turns to the left but is interrupted by a fence.

Bananas farm

In a while a farm can be seen across to the right, with fields of bananas.

Goat farm

Approximately 30 minutes from the start, the path becomes a little indistinct and descends slightly. Behind, the rocks of the Lara headland are plainly visible. Over to the right through the trees is a goat farm.

Soon the path disappears into the *maquis* and the way ahead is barred. Turn right to reach a cairn halfway up the slope, leading to another by a farm track. Keep straight ahead where a track goes off to the right and then turn steadily back to the gorge until running almost parallel to the sea.
Continue climbing parallel to the gorge until some low stone walls are encountered.

Final cairn

Skirt the solid barrier of *maquis* by moving to the right and the final cairn can be seen directly up the slope. Note that this cairn is triangular and not circular.
Sit down and enjoy the marvellous view.

A likely fellow climber in the Aspros Gorge

Descent

Try to follow the path marked with cairns and red paint marks. Almost certainly it will be lost, so head in the direction of Geronisos Island. Swing south when faced with barriers of bushes. In 15 minutes the cart track above the goat farm will be reached.

Pass to the right of the farm. After some five minutes the second farm is reached through fields of crops. Immediately after the building take the track that swings left, currently passing between banana fields. (The paths through the banana plantation could well look different. If the route is lost, keep heading towards the sea, and eventually you'll reach the road from Agios Georgios.)

The path again veers to the left, and soon there is a fork. However, keep to the right and then straight ahead. After ten minutes a T-junction is reached.

Turn right along a brown cart track through the banana plantation, swinging left to the cairn by the ravine. Descend to the bridge and cross the gorge to retrace the route to the start.

Agios Georgios

Agios Georgios is a tranquil place, but is becoming busier year by year. There is a distinctive domed church right on the shore, a taverna and a shed, a small beach and a harbour. The last receives small boats carrying holidaymakers from Pafos to Lara Beach of turtle fame. In the cliffs above the beach are numerous ancient tombs cut out of the solid rock.

A short distance offshore is the barren rock of **Geronisos Island** with relics of a Neolithic settlement and Roman buildings.

On the cliff top, slightly inland, stand the ruins of a 6th-century basilica, together with buildings of the 11th to 14th centuries. Several mosaics can be found close by.

On the coast, 25km (15½ miles) north of Pafos.

Agiou Neofytou Monastery

This is an intriguing and much-visited complex in hilly country at the very head of a wooded valley.

The monastery was founded at the beginning of the 12th century by the hermit Agios Neofytos, a native of Lefkara. He is said to have hewn with his own hands the three caves in the hillside. One was the church, another the sanctuary and the third his own dwelling place. The walls and ceilings are decorated with paintings, several of which were carried out under his supervision. In his cave there are alcoves and recesses where he kept his pens and papers. It was here that he wrote several books. One title, *Concerning the Misfortunes of Cyprus*, is about the conditions on the island in the 12th century. Another work, *Ritual Ordinance*, reveals his knowledge of early Greek monasticism.

The monastery has grown over the years and the present buildings around the courtyard are 15th century. A flight of steps leads up to the church with its three aisles and barrel-vaulted roof. There are 16th-century murals in the apse and some icons of the same period have survived. High in the aisle vaulting are some older murals.

Neofytos's remains still lie in the church, his bones in a wooden sarcophagus, his skull in a silver receptacle.

9km (5½ miles) north of Pafos. Open: Apr–Oct daily 9am–1pm & 2–6pm; Nov–Mar daily 9am–1pm & 2–4pm. Admission charge for some areas.

Akamas

The Akamas (*see p111*) is a splendid 155sq-km (60sq-mile) area of hills and rocky shores, and a habitat for species of flora and fauna unique to the Mediterranean. Some areas are now officially protected and parts of it isolated and peaceful. Only a few dirt tracks penetrate the peninsula, although nature trails have been established for walkers.

30km (18½ miles) northwest of Pafos.

Fontana Amorosa

This must be one of the remotest attractions on the island. In reality, it is little more than a goat well, and if it must be seen then it can be picked off during a trip to the splendid Akamas (*see above*). Cypriots say that whoever drinks from it will fall in love. This may once have been true, but today the water is not safe to drink.

Near Cape Arnaoutis at the west end of Chrysochou Bay.

Geroskipou

The village of 2,650 inhabitants, now really an outer suburb of Pafos, gets its name from the words *Hieros-Kepos*, meaning 'Holy Gardens of Aphrodite'. Although there are remains of a Roman temple, the town is probably of Byzantine origin. Despite its Folk Art Museum and famous church, Geroskipou would claim that its most important offering is its *Loukoumi*, or Turkish Delight.

The west

The 15th-century courtyard of Agiou Neofytou Monastery

Walk: Akamas

This is a clear-weather route for experienced walkers.

Allow 3½ hours for brisk walking and at least another hour in hot weather when plenty of liquids should be taken. Distance 10.5km (6½ miles). Ascent 400m (1,310ft).

The start at the Loutra Afroditis (Baths of Aphrodite) coincides with the tourist office's more direct nature trail. The route proceeds northwest to find an indistinct path lost in the hillside. To the left is the exit of a narrow valley. The path becomes clearer as the route moves up and to the right, to follow the right-hand side of the valley.

Plateau of the Magpies

After ten minutes a flat plateau, dotted with trees, is reached. There is easy walking on the left-hand perimeter, and after a further five minutes, a track leading to the right should be taken.

Very soon the path divides and the right fork must be taken. At this point the middle of the plateau is being crossed, and the walker is moving parallel to the sea and in the direction of a distant and flat-topped hill.

Deserted farm

To the left, about 400m (440yds) away, is the first of a group of abandoned buildings. A little later the path swings to the left and heads straight for what was once, perhaps, a goat farm, now a ruin, with lizards in its broken walls. To the right is a cave, and the path climbs to a cairn marked number 7.

Brown path on a white hill

To the left, a valley runs out on to the hill. Brown-stained rocks mark the climb up a hill. As the path moves towards the valley on the left, take the right fork, and climb up. You may be confused by the number of paths in front of you; press on until the path you are on comes out to run flat along the valley lip.

Forest glade

Keep a level course, going generally northwest through the trees, and eventually join a broad path. Keep straight on, climbing slowly. Soon there will be wooden markers specifying the flora. One will have the number B32. Follow the markers through the pine trees. When the main track swings to the left take the white stony path in front.

Welcome view

At the top of the rise the sea comes reassuringly into sight and with a few more steps the welcome view of the flat-topped hill. Now the way up the great hill can be clearly seen.

Before the hill can be climbed, there is a ten-minute descent to another forest glade, a crossroads of tracks complete with a drinking fountain, some seats and the trail 'gate'. At the signpost take the Aphrodite direction and see the ruined church (Pyrgos tis Rigenas) across the way. In a while, a track comes in from the right, but keep straight on up to turn sharply and climb the hill.

Summit

The path skirts the mountain top before descending. To reach the summit of Vakhines, follow the distinctive brown path between the white rocks. In a few minutes the high plateau is conquered, with the Akamas far below. It is surely the finest view in the whole of Cyprus.

Descent

The only safe way off the top is to return to the shoulder and follow the descending path along the northeastern face. Height is lost rapidly and 20 minutes will see you down to the track that runs along the shore from the Baths to Cape Arnaoutis. The Baths are about 25 minutes from this point.

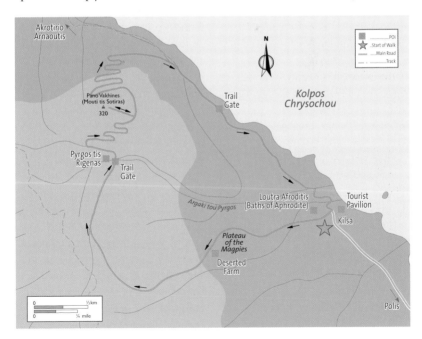

Agia Paraskevi

Five tiled domes on ancient stone walls make the church impressively picturesque and as interesting as any of the Byzantine churches of Cyprus. From within, it can be seen that three of the domes are over the nave and intersect with the two over the aisles, forming a Byzantine cross. A small chapel is built into the thick walls of the southeast corner. The church has undergone various changes over the years and was extended in the 19th century, and again more recently.

A clue to when the church was built can be gained from the 9th-century decorations over the altar. Other paintings are of the 10th century and there is a 12th-century *Dormition of the Virgin*. However, the paintings in the aisles are later, mainly of the 15th century. Geroskipou Folk Art Museum is close by (*see below*).

Geroskipou village, 3km (2 miles) east of Pafos. Tel: 26 961 859. Open: Apr–Oct Mon–Sat 8am–1pm & 2–5pm; Nov–Mar Mon–Sat 8am–1pm & 2–4pm.

Fresh Turkish Delight (*Loukoumi*)

LOUKOUMI

Geroskipou is the home of *Loukoumi*, or Turkish Delight. Anything Turkish is out of favour with some Greek Cypriots, so shops advertise it as Cyprus Delight. The name may have changed, but the product is still a mouthwatering confection of jelly, almonds, sugar and starch, dredged for good measure with icing sugar. It is an absolute must for visitors with a sweet tooth. Once upon a time there were two types, rose and almond flavoured. Today, it comes packaged in little boxes and in a multitude of varieties, including orange, kiwi and lemon. It can be found in the supermarkets but, of course, the ideal place to buy it is on Geroskipou's main street, where it is freshly made.

Geroskipou Folk Art Museum

Signposts direct visitors to this charming museum, an early 19th-century building that once belonged to the British vice-consul. On display are the work and tools of old-time silk-spinners, saddle-makers and other craftsmen.

3km (2 miles) east of Pafos. Tel: 26 306 216. Open: daily 8.30am–4pm. Admission charge.

Grivas Museum

A distinctive building houses the ship *Agios Georgios*, to mark the place near Chlorakas where General Grivas landed in 1954 to start his bloody EOKA campaign against the British. Grivas used the place more than once, for in 1955 the British seized the *Agios Georgios* carrying arms, just out to sea. During this escapade, Grivas himself came very close to capture, an outcome which might have spared the island the turmoil that followed.

The museum is worth a detour. *By the beach, 6.5km (4 miles) north of Pafos near Chlorakas, below the red-domed church. Open: at reasonable hours, normally daily. Free admission.*

Kolpos Lara (Lara Bay)

The beaches at Lara are splendid, with two sandy sections on either side of a bushy headland. The northern one is the more extensive. Here the coast faces due west, towards the open Mediterranean, and the waves tend to be bigger than elsewhere on the island.

Wonderful as the scenery is, Lara now has another claim to fame. Loggerhead turtles lay their eggs in the golden sands. The authorities are anxious that tourism should not frighten the turtles away from one of their last Mediterranean habitats, and to this end they have created a hatchery at Lara. Turtles are also kept in cages in Pafos harbour for releasing on the western coast. There may just be hope for the poor creatures as access to these shores by land is poor, the track from Agios Georgios being rough for cars. This, however, is good news for the boatmen of Pafos, for they bring crowds of visitors to the beaches every day. However, it is forbidden to use beach umbrellas as they could damage the turtle nests.

27km (17 miles) north of Pafos.

Loutra Afroditis (Baths of Aphrodite)

A trickle of water flows into a pool beneath a canopy of trees, a pleasantly cool place in summer, and supposedly where Aphrodite took a bath before her marriage. The nearby beach provides ideal conditions for swimmers and paddlers. On the cliffs is a tourist pavilion, overlooking Chrysochou Bay. There are several marked walking trails nearby.

8km (5 miles) west of Polis. Open: normally daily. Free admission.

The west

Tranquil Chrysochou Bay near the Baths of Aphrodite

Marion

This archaeological site features regularly in the official tourist literature and appears on many maps. However, the visitor will be sorely tried in attempting to find these celebrated ruins near Polis. The little that remains is from the town founded by the Athenians in the 7th century BC. It grew rich on copper until destroyed by the Ptolemies in 312 BC. When a new town was built it was called Arsinoe.

Immediately to the north of Polis. Open: daily. Free admission.

Ormos Korallion (Coral Bay)

There are, in fact, two sandy bays here, separated by crumbling white cliffs. The sea is calm and inviting, and sunbeds can be hired if real comfort is desired. Watersports are the order of the day, and paragliders operate from a floating platform.

It has to be said that because of the development, the area is no longer as splendid as it once was. Many of the houses overlooking the bay are the homes of Britons who retired there for a quiet life, only to find tourism hard on their heels. On the headland between the bays is a late Bronze Age site called **Maa-Palaeokastro**. Migrants from the Aegean built a settlement here in the 13th century BC.

13km (8 miles) north of Pafos.

Palaepaphos

Palaepaphos was the original Pafos. The Pafos we know today on the west coast was founded 1,200 years later. To avoid confusion, the names Nea (New) Pafos and Palae (Old) Pafos came into use.

The ruins of Palaepaphos (Aphrodite's Temple) lie on a limestone hillside in the village of Kouklia, overlooking the sea. It was clearly a large settlement but unfortunately only an incomplete record of its history has survived the passing years. A solid, well-built Lusignan manor house serves as a museum.

A sanctuary was constructed for the worship of Aphrodite, who, it was held, had risen from the sea at nearby Petra tou Romiou. It became the most famous of Aphrodite's shrines in antiquity.

However, the building of Nea Pafos to the west signalled the end of Palaepaphos's days of authority. A decline set in, and when the Romans came to Cyprus in 58 BC, only the splendour of the sanctuary remained.

To the west of the site are extensive Roman ruins; to the east the city wall runs along the ridge above a necropolis.

Manor house

The Château de Cavocle was built by the Lusignans in the 13th century. Only the east and south wings survive from the original building; the rest, including the imposing gate tower, are Ottoman. The restored building serves as a fascinating museum and storerooms for artefacts and other finds.

From the existing courtyard, steps lead down to the level of a medieval one. Here, a large cross-vaulted hall, 30m (98ft) long and 7m (23ft) wide, is lit by several pointed arch windows. This is a fine example of Frankish profane architecture. When the Ottomans took over Cyprus in the middle of the 16th century, the manor was extended and became the *chiftlik* (farmhouse).

Sanctuary of Aphrodite

This is the most interesting of the ruins on the site and is close to the museum. Here, unlike other temples on the island, the goddess was not represented as a human figure but as a conical stone.

THE CAPTURE OF PAFOS

When the Persian army attacked Palaepaphos in 498 BC they were determined to break through the city walls, and a great fight ensued. A ramp was raised and huge wooden towers shielding groups of soldiers were moved remorselessly up it to sweep away the defenders. But it was not to be so easy. The Pafians undermined the ramp with four tunnels, then burnt away the props with devastating results. In the end, however, the Persians prevailed and forced open the gate.

Next to the sanctuary is the 12th-century **Katholiki Church**, formerly called Panagia Chrysopolitissa, which served the original Byzantine village, built around the ruins of the ancient city.

The west

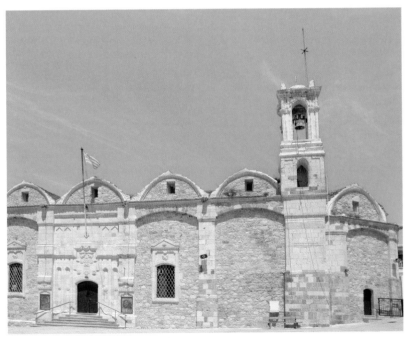

Pegeia's attractive Greek Orthodox church

To the south is the late Bronze Age **Sanctuary I**, dating from 1200 BC. **Roman Sanctuary II** in the north was built at about the same time but was damaged in an earthquake and abandoned in the 7th century AD.

Some 400m (440yds) to the west of the sanctuary is the **Roman Peristyle House**, built in the 1st century AD. In the peristyle itself several interesting mosaics of geometric pattern are preserved.

To the northwest is the **House of Leda**, another Roman building. Here the mosaic pavement of the *triclinium* (summer dining room), dating from the late 2nd century, was found. It is almost completely preserved with Leda and the swan depicted on it.

To the northeast of the manor house, and some 600m (660yds) northeast of Kouklia village (on the way to Arkimandrita), is Marcello Hill and the siege works, together with the site of the northeast gate. Excavations have revealed elaborate siege and counter-siege works, constructed during a Persian attack in 498 BC.

14km (9 miles) east of Pafos, signposted 'Sanctuary of Aphrodite'.
Tel: 26 432 155. Open: Fri–Wed 9am–4pm, Thur 8am–5pm. Admission charge.

Panagia Chryseleousa

This structure is a simple 12th-century design, originally of the cruciform type and complete with a dome. Later additions include a domed narthex.

There are many paintings to see, in various states of preservation. The 15th-century decoration of the main dome is visible and is generally in good condition. There is a Venetian shield by the east wall and a carved wooden iconostasis from the 16th century. *Empa village, 3km (2 miles) north of Pafos. A local shopkeeper holds the key.*

Pegeia (Pageia)

This village presents its best face to visitors approaching from Pafos. Unfortunately, the lovely dark poplars are now obscured by the holiday homes of expatriates. They now cover the hillsides that rise into the hazy distance. Byzantine origins have been claimed for the village, but no one can be sure of this. To the west of the main square and at a lower level is a public area with an ancient barrel-vaulted chamber which collects Pegeia's famous spring water. Indeed, the word *peyia* in Greek-Cypriot dialect has the meaning 'source of water'. In recent years the village has seen the development of retirement and holiday homes for Britons. There are several low-priced restaurants providing Greek food as enjoyed by the locals.
16km (10 miles) north of Pafos.

Petra tou Romiou (Aphrodite's Birthplace)

These white rocks in a blue sea are spectacular. Folklore recounts that

Cyprus's favourite daughter, Aphrodite, was born in the sea foam by the rocks. Today there is still plenty of foam as the water swirls around the shore and runs up the shingly beach. It is a favourite stopping place for many. In late afternoon, the view over the rocks from the high ground to the east is memorable. A few metres inland is a tourist pavilion serving snacks and providing a good view over the rocks. *24km (15 miles) southeast of Pafos.*

Polis

A popular tourist town, Polis nevertheless remains a lovely, laid-back seaside community. The charming village square is pedestrianised and the one-way system traps visiting motorists, causing mayhem, which the locals don't seem to mind a bit. Barmen have a way of getting lost among the customers, but, when discovered, will generously serve you with as many drinks as you request.

Once popular with backpackers, Polis sees a moneyed set, staying at the nearby Anassa, filling its café tables. To the west, a few kilometres away, **Latchi** has an attractive fishing harbour and superb seafood tavernas. Polis campsite is due north of the town, close to the beach. *Chrysochou Bay.*

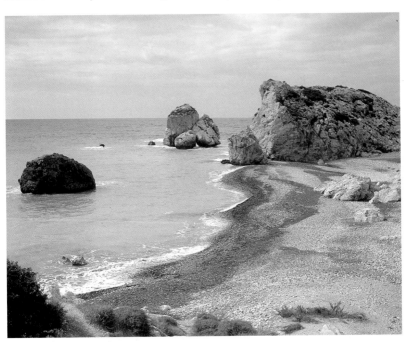

Petra tou Romiou, Aphrodite's Birthplace

Greek orthodoxy

Christianity first came to Cyprus in AD 45 when apostles Paul and Barnabas spread the doctrine with some success. Nevertheless, it was not until the imperial recognition of Christianity by Constantine the Great in AD 313 that the persecuted religion emerged from the catacombs. By the end of the century the Church of Cyprus was fully established with bishops in all the main towns. The kingships of antiquity were replaced by bishoprics and the old temples to pagan gods by basilican churches dedicated to Christ, the Virgin Mary and the saints.

During the centuries of Byzantine control, the Church, which had become ecclesiastically independent in its early days, continued to develop.

In 1192, the coming of the Lusignans established the Latin Church on the island, resulting in a long struggle for survival by the Orthodox Church. Its bishoprics were reduced and the remaining prelates banished to remote villages.

Ottoman domination after 1571 resulted in the Latin Church being suppressed and its great cathedrals being turned into mosques. However, the Turks were liberal to the Orthodox

The peaceful courtyard of Kykkos Monastery

Church and the archbishop acquired great power.

The Greek Cypriots are still a religious people, not in any dramatic way, but simply as a natural part of their lives. Many churches are being built, reflecting the new-found wealth of the island.

Monastic life

Monasticism grew out of Constantine's unification of state

and Church. In Cyprus the life of renunciation was often a solitary existence, although in some areas communities of monks were established as early as the 7th century. Very few of these monasteries have survived; most of the buildings we see today were founded in the 12th and 13th centuries. Even these had humble beginnings. That they grew at all was the result of donations by royalty. They are impressive constructions with tranquil cloisters and courtyards.

In the early days the monks lived terribly frugal lives, though this spartan existence had its attractions. A community could be as many as 400. However, by the end of the 19th century, a monastery as important as Kykkos found its numbers had dwindled to 90. Today, even with electricity, drainage and other comforts, the monasteries retain only a fraction of this number, and it is still falling. Older monks now worry that modern Cypriots might reject religion in the same unquestioning way by which they earlier held it. Even so, the monks believe fervently in a revival, and in the interim they carry on with their prayers and the traditional occupations of farming, making jam and wine, and bee-keeping.

A monk painting a traditional icon

The Troodos

The Troodos Mountains dominate much of the island. If one includes all the land above 300m (984ft), then it would account for well over one-third of the land mass. In the northwest the foothills come right down to the sea and a spur runs out into the Akamas Peninsula. Central Troodos descends rapidly to the central plain to the north, and more gradually to Lemesos (Limassol) in the south. The northeastern flanks approach to within 24km (15 miles) of Lefkosia (Nicosia).

The highest of the igneous rocks, thrust up by the action of continental plates in prehistory, is known as Mount Olympos, reaching to 1,952m (6,404ft) above sea level. This elevated ground extends east for 40km (25 miles) before descending to more modest heights. Despite their impressive stature, these are not wild mountains; villages and roads can be found near all but the very highest peaks.

In the west and parts of central Troodos the slopes are pine-clad. Golden oak and willow are found in the valleys, and where there is insufficient rainfall for trees the *maquis* colonises the rocky slopes. In June and July the highest ground turns yellow as the dense dwarf shrubs come into flower.

The valleys and folds of the hills conceal a great number of villages, Prodromos being the highest at 1,390m

Prodromos, the highest village in Cyprus

(4,560ft) above sea level. Many have a somewhat ramshackle appearance, for they are largely working places, some untouched by tourism. Even those on the tourist route up the Solea Valley have the same characteristics as they perch precariously on the hillside. The buildings are quite different from those in the arid flatlands. Roofs have a steep pitch and are covered with red tiles and sometimes corrugated metal sheets. It is for good reason, as the winter is wet with snow on higher ground. There are, however, many clear days when the hills stand out in sharp relief as they never do in the hazy summer. Indeed, from the north ski slope of Olympos the view over Güzelyurt (Morfou) Bay and out across the sea to the snow-capped Toros Mountains of Turkey is a memorable sight.

Kellaki, a hillside village near Eptagoneia

Troodos is famous for its spring water, which is bottled and sold island-wide. It is also a notable fruit-growing area; the people of the Solea Valley and Marathasa regions specialise in cherries, apples, pears and plums. Grapes are grown everywhere in Cyprus but nowhere better than on the southern slopes of the Troodos. The luxuriant grape crop is collected in villages such as Omodos and carried down to Lemesos (Limassol) where it is turned into one of the many Cypriot wines. The mountains are naturally colder than the lowlands, although in high summer the temperatures still reach 30°C (86°F) and the sun is intense. As a result, the hill resorts are a popular

destination for the Cypriots, who spend the weekend or longer in places like Kakopetria or Platres.

Hillwalking is popular and the Cyprus tourist organisation has prepared several trails through the pine woods. However, the heat of summer has to be reckoned with, and away from the trails the impenetrable *maquis* makes for slow progress.

An important feature of the region is the monasteries and the numerous Byzantine churches that hide in the valleys. These cloistered retreats are splendid places for half-day visits, as they contain a wealth of wall paintings, many of them the best and most complete in Cyprus.

Agia Moni

The original monastery was built in the 6th century on the foundations of an ancient pagan temple. However, the buildings seen today were constructed between 1638 and 1820. It is set in an idyllic location, high in the hills, surrounded by

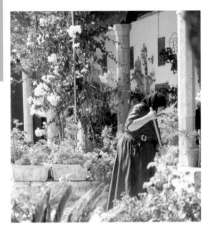

Working in the garden at Agios Irakleidios

pine trees and fruit orchards, and although closed to the public, it is worth a visit for the magnificent views alone.
40km (25 miles) northwest of Lemesos.

Agios Ioannis Lampadistis

One of the most interesting ecclesiastical monuments in Cyprus. Its origins are Byzantine, the cross-in-square church dating from the 11th century. Two other churches are of the 15th century. The rebuilt barrel-vaulted church is the one dedicated to St John himself. A tremendous roof of tiles now protects the buildings.

Some early decoration, probably of the 11th century, was discovered recently. However, the best paintings are from the 13th century and include the *Triumphal Entry of Christ into Jerusalem.*

The olive and wine presses on the ground floor of the east wing are worth

a look. The treasury in the west wing is also interesting.

One of the biggest religious fairs in the valley is held in the village of Kalopanagiotis (*see pp102–3*) on Agios Ioannis's (St John's) Day, 4 October. *Kalopanagiotis, 55km (34 miles) northwest of Lemesos. Open: Mar–May & Sept Tue–Sat 9.30am–5pm, Sun 11am–5pm; Jun–Aug Tue–Sat 9am–1pm, Sun 11am–1pm & 3–7pm; Oct–Feb Tue–Sat 10am–3.30pm, Sun 11am–3.30pm.*

Agios Irakleidios Monastery

Although the present buildings date only from 1773, this monastery was founded in Byzantine times. A community of nuns is ensconced here and they nurture the wonderful gardens as well as selling almond honey and other confections. Inside the church the iconostasis contains the icon of John the Baptist, which is 150 years older than the church building. Agios Irakleidios (St Heraclides) conducted St Paul and St Barnabas to nearby Tamassos during their missionary travels. He was killed by pagans and buried on the site of the old monastery. In fact, his skull is still kept in a casket in the church.
19km (12 miles) southwest of Lefkosia, a little beyond Politiko. Open: daily, but closed to visitors from noon to 3pm.

Agios Nikolaos tis Stegis

The unusual name (which means 'St Nicholas of the Roof') comes from the huge roof of this church. Nearly all the churches of the Troodos Mountains have pitched roofs, but this one is bigger and better than all the others. It is covered with flat tiles that protect the lower domed roof. The original church was constructed in the 11th century, with a narthex and cupola being added in the 12th century. Inside are some fine frescoes, many dating from the time the church was built and some as late as the 17th century. *The Nativity* is from the 14th century, and *The Transfiguration* much earlier.

3.2km (2 miles) southwest of the village of Kakopetria. Open: Tue–Sat 9am–4pm, Sun 11am–4pm. Closed: Mon.

Asinou (Panagia Forviotissa)

This little building, the finest of Cyprus's painted churches, is a UNESCO World Heritage-listed site on a north-facing hillside; it's surrounded by eucalyptus trees. The external appearance is unusual; the walls are solid stone, as to be expected, but the roof has a steep double pitch with a

This wall features scenes from the Second Coming, early 13th century. Remarkable Byzantine frescoes decorate the interior of Asinou Church

The Troodos

clay tile covering. This feature is merely the traditional weather shield to protect the domes and barrel vaults below. Asinou is an old church dating from 1105, although the dome and narthex were added in 1200.

The frescoes inside are remarkable, an impressive record of Byzantine and post-Byzantine art from the building of the church to the 16th century. They all merit inspection. In the centre of the apse is the *Coming of the Apostles*. In the west bay above the door is the *Dormition of the Virgin Mary*, and in the lunette above is painted the *Entry of Christ into Jerusalem*. The south apse has three outstanding paintings: *St George Mounted*, *St Anastasia* and the *Mother of God*.
40km (25 miles) southwest of Lefkosia. Open: May–Aug daily 9.30am–5pm; Sept–Oct daily 9.30am–4.30pm; Nov–Apr daily 9.30am–4pm. There is usually a caretaker present, but, if not, the priest with the key is at Nikitari, 5km (3 miles) away, and he is happy to accompany visitors to the church (tel: 99 830 329).

Fikardou

This whole village has been declared an ancient monument to safeguard its 18th-century houses. Many have remarkable woodwork features. The restored dwellings of **Katsinioros** and **Achilleas Demetri** have parts surviving from the 16th century, and received the Europa Nostra award in 1987.
35km (22 miles) southwest of Lefkosia.

Kakopetria

The village sits at a height of 670m (2,200ft) in the wooded Solea Valley, halfway up the northern slopes of Mount Olympos. From the main road the houses come suddenly into view – picturesque, but ramshackle. The village's name means 'bad stone'. According to legend there used to be a stone on the hill above the village, which brought good luck. However, one day, a newly married couple went to receive the blessing of the stone, which then changed its character, rolled over and crushed them.

This historic little village is thought to be so typical of Cyprus that the buildings in the older part of the village have been restored and preservation orders placed on them.

Although a holiday resort, it is mainly a haunt of the locals. Most days the main square, with its political graffiti on the walls, presents a typical Cypriot village scene with crowds of people at the café tables in animated conversation.

There are several small hotels and restaurants, and a market.
56km (35 miles) southwest of Lefkosia.

Kalopanagiotis

This village is situated high on the northern slopes of the western Troodos. It is a summer resort and best known for its sulphur springs, which rise on the eastern side of the valley. There are three springs and the temperature of the water varies

The village of Kakopetria, nestling in the wooded Solea Valley of Mount Olympos, has a population of about 2,000

with each, an assortment of medical treatments being claimed for the differing degrees of warmth. Apparently 21°C (70°F) works wonders for general debility and nervous depression. A short distance down the valley is the Kalopanagiotis Dam, an idyllic spot for a picnic. Also near the village is the Agios Ioannis Lampadistis Monastery (*see p100*).
55km (34 miles) northwest of Lemesos.

Kykkos

This monastery is the most celebrated in Cyprus and known throughout the Orthodox world. It is surrounded by pine trees in the clear air of 1,318m (4,324ft) above sea level, cool in summer, and cold during the winter nights.

Kykkos was founded in about 1100 by a hermit called Isaiah, in the reign of the Byzantine emperor Alexios Comnenus. To mark the foundation and in gratitude for his daughter being cured of sciatica, he presented Isaiah with an icon of the Virgin Mary. This was one of only three painted by St Luke and a very special gift. It has not been seen for centuries and is covered by a silver plate embossed with a reproduction of the Virgin, the original being too sacred for the human eye to gaze upon. It is also believed to have rain-making powers. The faithful consider that the bowed pine trees on the mountain top have taken up this configuration out of reverence to the icon.

Nearby, visitors will see a bronze arm, withered it seems, and allegedly once the flesh of an infidel who interfered with one of the lamps illuminating the icon.

GRIGORIS AFXENTIOU

A short distance from the Kykkos Monastery, down a forest track, is the cave where Grigoris Afxentiou was trapped during the EOKA uprising. Second in command to Grivas, he was determined not to surrender. The British forces were equally determined to capture him, but after a corporal was shot dead they tried to flush out their man by pouring petrol into the entrance and firing an explosive charge. Afxentiou, although badly burnt, actually died of a bullet through the head, perhaps suicide, or an exploding round set off by the heat.

Despite the powers of the icon, the monastery has suffered several catastrophes. It was burnt down in 1365 and replaced by a wooden structure that then suffered the same fate in 1542. In 1751 it was burnt down again, and likewise in 1831. The famous golden icon miraculously survived each fiery disaster.

Over the centuries the monastery has enjoyed great authority in the Greek Orthodox world. Pilgrims brought gifts and money, and property was gained in Asia Minor, Greece and even Russia. Today, the monastery depends entirely on revenues from its property in Cyprus for its upkeep.

During the EOKA campaign against the British in the 1950s, the monastery was used by the guerrillas for communications and the handling of supplies. Inside is one of the finest museums on the island, full of icons, ceremonial gowns and ancient pottery. The hill of Throni is close by (*see p109*).

Visitors to this monastery, as indeed to all churches and monasteries in Cyprus, should be modestly dressed. *61km (38 miles) northwest of Lemesos. Tel: 22 942 435. Open: Jun–Oct daily 10am–6pm; Nov–May daily 10am–4pm. Admission charge to museum.*

Machaira Monastery is beautifully located in the Machairas Mountains

Machaira

This monastery was founded in 1148 by two monks who had come to the island. Later, the Byzantine emperor Manuel Comnenus, much taken by the place, granted the monastery a large tract of mountainside and an annual donation. Thus encouraged, the small community extended the accommodation, and in 1172 it acquired its first abbot. During the plague at the end of the 14th century, King James I of Cyprus and his entire court took refuge there.

In 1530, much of the complex was destroyed in a fire and suffered the same fate in 1892. When rebuilding was carried out, little from the past was retained. The present design is unusual, with large buttresses to the external walls and balconies.

There are various suggestions for the derivation of the name Machaira, which means 'knife'. One that may surprise hot summer visitors is that it is a reference to an icy cutting wind. The drive through this fine country makes the visit all the more worthwhile.
Eastern Troodos, 48km (30 miles) southwest of Lefkosia. Tel: 22 359 334. Open: Mon–Fri 8.30am–5.30pm. Closed: Sat & Sun.

Mount Olympos

The mountain is the highest in Cyprus, at 1,952m (6,404ft) above sea level, just high enough to catch the winter snow. It piles up to a great depth, but once the sun comes out the ensuing thaw is

The monk Ignatios was told in a dream to build the Chrysorrogiatissa Monastery

rapid. The summit is no rocky pyramid, merely a rounded dome clothed fairly sparingly with pine trees. A road runs to the top to service the radar domes controlled by the British military and some Cypriot installations. These blight the scenery and today there is no access to the summit slopes and the magnificent views over Güzelyurt Bay and Turkey. The whole area is now a winter playground with several ski lifts, although the ski shop and café are as dilapidated as ever (*see pp167–8*).
45km (28 miles) north of Lemesos.

Panagia Chrysorrogiatissa

The monastery lies high on the western slopes of the Troodos. It was founded in 1152 by a monk called Ignatios, having been told in a dream by the

Virgin Mary to build it on this site. Alternative versions claim that Ignatios found an icon of the Virgin, painted by St Luke, and that this prompted him to construct the church. The monastery then went through turbulent times. It was totally destroyed in 1770 to punish the monks who had shown political sympathy for an uprising on the Greek mainland. The buildings we see today therefore date from the 19th century, although due to a fire in 1967, parts were rebuilt much more recently.

The monastery's political fortunes took a further savage turn in 1956 when the abbot was shot in his room by two men dressed as monks, acting on a false report that he had betrayed two EOKA members.

The demure translation of the monastery's name is 'our lady of the golden pomegranate'. Various rival versions are put forward, however, including 'our lady of the golden nipple'.

The monastery is built around a courtyard with the church in the centre. It contains various relics, including the original icon, now covered by silver.

The monks are also expanding the attractions of the monastery, offering the services of an icon painter, and selling books and their own wine (recommended). Within the premises, the Icons and Utensils Treasury is open to the public.

There is also a café adjacent to the monastery, with extensive views of the surrounding hills.

34km (21 miles) northeast of Pafos.

Open: May–Aug daily 9.30am–12.30pm & 1.30–6.30pm; Sept–Apr daily 10am–12.30pm & 1.30–4pm. Admission charge to Treasury.

Panagia Eleousa and Panagia Theotokos

Both of these fascinating small churches stand in the Solea Valley, below the village of Galata. Panagia Eleousa was built in 1502, and contains paintings of the Italian Byzantine style. Panagia Theotokos (Church of the Archangel Michael) is close by and even smaller. They are survivors from the Monastery of Podithou that once occupied the site. Both churches are normally locked and enquiries for the keys should be made in Galata.

54km (34 miles) southwest of Lefkosia, 1.5km (1 mile) below Kakopetria.

Panagia tou Araka (Lagoudera Church)

Built in 1190, this church is typical of the mid-Byzantine period, having a vaulted single aisle with three arched recesses in each of the side walls and a dome over the centre. A steep-pitched, tiled roof protects the dome and also a later enclosure in timber.

The marvellous wall paintings inside are some of the best on the island and make up a complete series. From the dome, Christ Pantocrator, ruler of the world, looks down from heaven, while in the arched north recess the *Presentation of the Virgin Mary* is displayed. Artists were commissioned

Interior of Panagia tou Araka

from Constantinople itself, capital of the Byzantine Empire. The unusually high level of workmanship invested in these frescoes has paid dividends in the modern world by attracting the protection of UNESCO World Cultural Heritage status to the establishment. *Lagoudera Troodos, 8km (5 miles) east of Kakopetria. The church is kept locked but the priest can be found in the house next door and will escort visitors.*

Pano Panagia

This small village, the birthplace of Makarios III, the first president of Cyprus, has become a modern-day centre of pilgrimage.

The house where the young Michalakis Mouskos grew up is open to the public. It is a humble, two-room abode, with his parents' bed in the middle of the first room. There are other relics from his family life, mainly pots, pans and a few pictures.

Just down the road in the main square is the Archbishop Makarios III Historical and Cultural Centre, displaying details of cultural events in Panagia as well as photos of significant moments in the archbishop's life. There are also items of clothing, scorched in the coup against him.

32km (20 miles) northeast of Pafos. House (tel: 26 722 255) and Centre (tel: 26 722 473) open: May–Sept daily 9am–1pm & 3–6pm (House 2–4pm); Oct–Apr daily 9am–1pm & 2–4pm. Admission charge.

Pano Platres

This well-known village lies partially hidden on a thickly wooded hillside at 1,100m (3,609ft) in the Troodos Mountains. It is smarter in appearance than the other hill resorts and has better facilities. It became popular as an escape from Lefkosia's heat and is claimed to be beneficial to those in need of a tonic. Because of the contours, the road configuration through the village is a nightmare for drivers in the dark. For pedestrians, access from one level to another is by exceedingly steep pathways.

There are several tracks for walkers in the surrounding woods where you can look out over the vineyards to the distant south coast and the Akrotiri Peninsula. The Kaledonia Falls, 3.2km (2 miles) to the north, make an idyllic picnic spot.

South of Mount Olympos, 34km (21 miles) from Lemesos (Limassol).

Peristerona Church

Some licence has been taken in including this 10th-century church in the Troodos section for it is in the centre of the village of Peristerona, on the west bank of the boulder-strewn Peristerona River.

Its five domes are rivalled in Cyprus only by the church at Geroskipou. They are set over the nave and one above each of the side aisles. Below the domes pierced openings separate the two sections. The narthex is a later addition. Of interest is the icon

The domed church of Peristerona

of the *Presentation of Christ in the Temple* and an old chest embellished with a scene from the Siege of Rhodes. *Peristerona, 27km (17 miles) west of Lefkosia. Enquiries for the key should be made in the village.*

Stavros tou Agiasmati

The church is found on the northern slopes of the central Troodos. The church itself forms a simple rectangle but a surrounding protective wall and roof render it barely visible. Unfortunately, visitors have to traverse 4km (2½ miles) of unmade road to reach the church, which is kept locked.

Enquiries for the key must be made in Platanistasa village. However, the effort is well rewarded, for this modest building contains one of the finest series of wall paintings on religious themes in Cyprus. Among them are

The Last Supper, The Washing of the
Feet and *The Betrayal.*
Central Troodos, 5km (3 miles)
northwest of Platanistasa.

Tamassos

Tamassos was one of the oldest city
kingdoms in Cyprus, dating from
about 2500 BC. It gained its prosperity
from copper exports.

Excavations began in 1874 and
three underground tombs were found,
possibly belonging to early kings of
Tamassos. The tombs were looted a
long time ago but the impressive
carvings and sculptures on the
structures themselves remain.

The site also embraces the remains
of a few houses, although they are
difficult to identify. The Agios
Irakleidios Monastery is close by
(*see p100*).
19km (12 miles) southwest of Lefkosia.
Open: Apr–Oct daily 9.30am–5pm;
Nov–Mar daily 8.30am–4pm.
Admission charge.

Throni

This is the name of a hill overlooking
Kykkos Monastery (*see pp103–4*). At the
very top is a famous icon in a small
chapel. President Makarios III was born
in the foothills of the western Troodos,
and asked to be buried close to the icon,
overlooking his favourite hills and
village of birth. He died unexpectedly,
with his resting place unfinished.
Bulldozers worked around the clock,
completing it just before the cortège

arrived from Lefkosia in a torrential
downpour. It is indeed a spectacular
burial place; from this vantage point the
whole of western Cyprus can be seen.
1.5km (1 mile) from Kykkos Monastery
in the western Troodos.

Trooditissa

This collection of buildings is found
high in the western Troodos. Although
the monastery, devoted to the Virgin
Mary, was established in the 10th
century, the present church dates from
1731. Inside is a famous icon of the
Virgin Mary, brought from Asia Minor
and plated with silver, and many
ecclesiastical treasures such as old
sanctuary doors and other items.

A large religious fair is held in the
grounds on 15 August for the
Assumption of the Virgin Mary.
Western Troodos, between the villages
of Pano Platres and Prodromos. This
is a place of prayer and not open to
the public.

This building, adjacent to the burial place of
Makarios III, houses a famous icon

Wildlife and conservation

Cyprus has some interesting wildlife. The much-vaunted mouflon (mountain sheep) has become a symbol of Cyprus, and features prominently in the official tourist literature. In reality, it exists only in very small numbers in the forests of western Cyprus and is only easily seen in enclosures in the Troodos.

High above the forest and out as far as the Akamas Peninsula, the griffon vulture is sometimes seen. However, for really good sightings of these astonishing birds with 2.5m (8ft) wingspans, the Beşparmak Mountains are the place.

The southern slopes are the home of the blunt-nosed viper. Climbers of the spiky Beşparmak Mountains sometimes have unwelcome face-to-face confrontations with the highly venomous ledge-dwelling reptile, which is also found at lower elevations in the maquis and forests.

Cyprus is visited every year by millions of migrating birds, many on their way to Africa. The eloquent-sounding Eleonora's falcon stays long enough to breed and can be seen on the cliffs at Cape Gata. However, the most notable and famous of Cyprus's feathered winter visitors is the greater flamingo, which takes up residence on the salt lakes of Larnaka and Akrotiri. The best known of the island's endemic birds is the locally breeding Cyprus warbler.

Kolpos Lara (Lara Bay) in the west is famous for its nesting loggerhead turtles. Tourism is the biggest threat to their survival, but foxes and crows kill vast numbers of hatchlings. At the opposite end of the island the sandy beaches of the Karpaz Yarımadası (Karpasia) Peninsula offer a better refuge to this endangered species.

The visitor cannot help but notice the lizard population, for the sun and

Flamingos at a salt lake in winter

The griffon vulture inhabits the Beşparmak Mountains

high temperatures provide an ideal climate. An impressive specimen is the starred agama, which grows to a length of 30cm (12in), living in rocks and stone walls. Even more striking, but not nearly as easy to find, is the common chameleon, renowned for its remarkable colour changes and incredible 360-degree vision.

Tourist development in Cyprus has brought great economic benefit, but at a price. On both sides of the Green Line, much of the coastline has changed forever. The west and north coastal areas are some of the last Mediterranean refuges of loggerhead turtles and monk seals. Turtles are being reared in Pafos harbour to be released on the western shores. These attempts to protect such endangered species are worthy, but, sadly, with the increase in visitors to this part of Cyprus, they may well prove ineffective.

The Friends of the Akamas

This environmental group was the first to start campaigning in Cyprus. The battleground became the Akamas Peninsula, which had escaped development because of its remoteness. The Friends succeeded in having the Akamas Forest declared a national park in 1989.

Development elsewhere on the peninsula is prohibited.

North Cyprus

Like the south, the occupied north has seen much uncontrolled development and its coastline and hinterland have suffered. However, at least part of the remote Karpaz Yarımadası (Karpasia) Peninsula remains relatively unspoilt.

Walk: Troodos

The 9.6km (6-mile) circuit north of Platres ascends 400m (1,312ft) and includes Kaledonia Falls. This is a more demanding excursion for experienced hillwalkers and should be attempted in good weather.

Allow 3¾ hours for brisk walking and at least another hour in hot weather, when plenty of liquids should be taken.

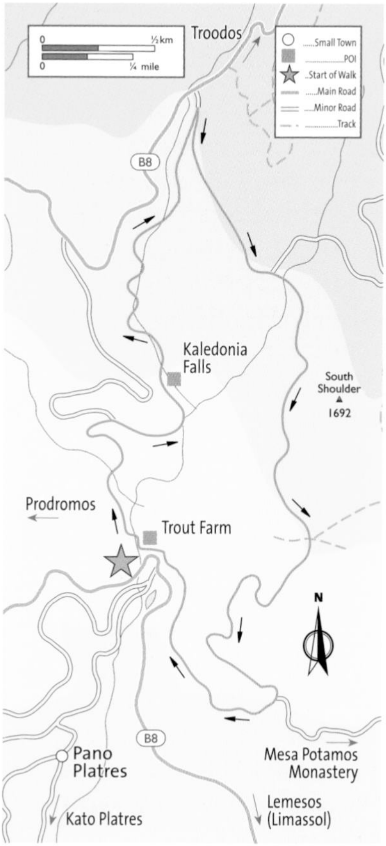

Start at the trout farm. Take the broad, concreted track signposted 'Kaledonia Falls 3km'. The route zigzags up the wooded hillside and passes a road off to the left. Ignore this and keep straight on as the signpost directs. Very soon a nature trail 'gate' is reached and the road left behind.

Kaledonia Falls

The famous falls can now be clearly heard, and in a few minutes they are reached. It is a cool spot that provides some relief after the climb.

Forest climb

When ready, return to the wooden steps marked 'Kryos Potamos' and ascend to the top of the falls. The path now stays with the stream, crossing and recrossing the bed. At regular intervals 'trail' posts advise the name of selected species of flora.

Twenty minutes after the falls, the stream bed becomes gorge-like and flattens out. Keep on climbing the main path and soon traffic will be heard from the road up to the left.

Right turn

Half an hour on from the falls a green hut will be seen on the right, with a car park up front, an ideal place to rest a while. From now on the route is less demanding, the main ascent being over.

Turn sharp right along the wide forest track and head into the trees. The early ground rises; the open views give an indication of splendours to come. Ten minutes (about 800m/880yds) after the right turn, when the road turns to the left, there is a pine-covered route off to the right. This *must* be taken; a green seat above the path will confirm that this is the right direction.

Splendid isolation

In a short while, the route throws off its disguise and there is no doubt that the path exists and is going somewhere. And it is, as it starts its magnificent descent. No motorbikes will be met here, no fellow visitors; glorious solitude is guaranteed. Initially, the path falls steadily and the head of a valley will be reached shortly after leaving the forest road. Now the path turns south into an area where crow-like birds flit silently through the trees. Down below, Pano Platres looks deceptively close.

Screes

Ten minutes from the upper trail 'gate' the path turns left with the bed of a dry

The gentle Kaledonia Falls

stream to the right. Cones are piled up underfoot and the route leaves the bed behind. In another ten minutes turn a bend affording spectacular views.

Needles and pines

Care is now required as the way is entirely covered with pine needles, disconcertingly slippery underfoot. At these lower altitudes the smell of pine is marvellously overpowering. Half an hour from the second trail 'gate', the path turns to the right and then doubles back on itself.

Diminishing return

This is an exceptional forest descent. Some distance on, the path is cut in two by a broad forestry department road. Care is needed to descend the steep upper embankment and to locate the continuing route on the far side.

An unmetalled road below is the first sign that the walk's end is imminent. Follow the path down till where it joins the road from the trout farm to Mesa Potamos Monastery. Turn right for the trout farm.

The north

This section covers all the territory north of the military line dividing the island (see pp14–15). It is an area under the control of the Turkish Cypriots, and has quite a different feel to the south, most notable in the landscape (less developed), architecture (more mosques) and cuisine (more Turkish than Greek).

While northern Cyprus is less populated than the south, it is attracting an increasing number of expats and holidaymakers (largely British) and the resulting villa and apartment developments. While this has been great for the economy, the things that initially attracted foreigners to the north – open spaces and pristine beaches – are rapidly disappearing.

Girne (Kyrenia) on the north coast gets busy with tourists, as does Gazimağusa in the east. The splendid beach at Varosha, however, once crowded with swimmers and sunbathers, has been empty since 1974, currently off-limits.

Some would say that the Turks have the best of the island's scenery. This is debatable, but certainly the Beşparmak Mountains are an impressive sight, extraordinary in that they traverse 90km (56 miles) of the northern littoral, yet nowhere are they more than 3km (2 miles) wide, a rocky backbone stretching from Lapta

(Lapithos) to Kantara and reaching heights of 1,000m (3,280ft) above sea level. The rock is limestone and marble, the slopes covered with cypresses and Aleppo pine.

The north coast boasts some good beaches. There is an abundance of sand in Güzelyurt in the west, a good beach by Salamis in the east and the country's most beautiful beaches on the Karpaz Yarımadası (Karpasia) Peninsula.

The central plain, Mesaoria, is contained entirely in the Turkish-Cypriot section. A midday drive through this summer wilderness is a hot affair of mirages and minor dusty whirlwinds. Few would believe that in springtime the land is transformed from a flat, bare plain into a blaze of colour with wild mustard, poppies, chrysanthemums and a hundred other species bursting forth.

Just as some Turkish names of villages were changed in the south, Greek place names have been changed by the authorities of the north. For example, Lapithos, a favourite haunt of Lawrence Durrell, is now Lapta, and Akanthou is Tatlısu. Nevertheless, should travellers using a Greek-Cypriot map inadvertently stray off the beaten track they will receive a cheerful and noisy welcome from the local children and an equally animated farewell.

The Karpaz Yarımadası (Karpasia) Peninsula, or 'Panhandle' as it is known, is another unique geographical feature. It reaches out towards Syria for nearly 80km (50 miles), yet is only a fraction of this in width, the blue sea on both shores being visible from high ground.

Along the shore are splendid beaches, together with several intriguing sites of antiquity. The area was once well populated and forested, with ships calling to collect cedarwood. Gradually, its importance declined, perhaps with a change of climate, and for centuries it has been remote and isolated, with much of it now protected.

Many significant Greek Orthodox churches have been allowed to become derelict in the north just as the many mosques in the south have since 1974, but these can still be admired for their beauty.

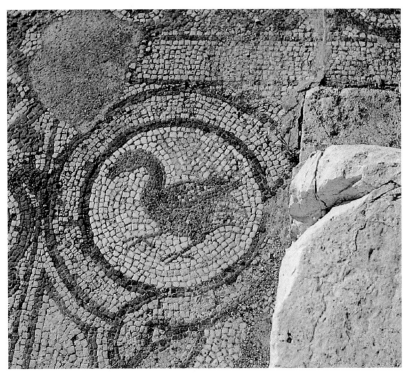

The Roman mosaic floors at Soloi basilica are well preserved

GAZIMAĞUSA (FAMAGUSTA)

Founded in the 11th century BC, Salamis was abandoned following earthquakes in AD 648, its population moving to present-day Gazimaĝusa. The Roman Cypriots were followed by Egyptians, Franks, Genoans and Venetians, remnants of their civilisations making the then Famagusta (Frankish for 'buried in the sand') a fascinating place. Today it's a lively university town with a growing expat population.

Agia Zoni and Agios Nikolaos

Agia Zoni is a small church built in the 15th century, dedicated to the Blessed Virgin Mary. It is designed in the form of a cross, with a central dome and barrel-vaulted roof. During the Ottoman siege of the town in 1570–71 it escaped damage. Inside are the remnants of wall paintings.

Nearby is 15th-century Agios Nikolaos. Part of the nave and the semicircular apse have survived.
Hisar Yolou Sokağı.

Biddulph's Gate

Named after Sir Robert Biddulph, British High Commissioner in Cyprus in 1879, who saved the monument from destruction, it is an imitation of a Roman triumphal arch, and probably marked the entrance to a merchant's house. Two large marble columns formed part of the gateway but are now gone.
Naim Efendi Sokağı.

Cafer Paşa Fountain and Turkish baths

Cafer Paşa was an Ottoman general and administrator who ordered the construction of water arches to supply the town with water. The original structure was destroyed; however, a replacement was built using the surviving fountainhead, bearing the date 1597 and the name Cafer Paşa. A boathouse built by the general in 1601 also survives.
Naim Efendi Sokağı, opposite Lala Mustafa Paşa Mosque.

Canbulat Museum

Fine examples of Turkish folk art, including embroidery and clothing, can be seen at this museum.
Canbulat Bastion in the walls. Open: Jun–Sept, Mon–Fri 9am–5pm; Oct–May, Mon–Fri 9am–1pm & 2–4.45pm. Closed: Sat & Sun. Admission charge.

Carmelite Church (St Mary's)

One of the most important churches, a monastery once stood on this site, although nothing remains. The ruined church dates from the mid-14th century, soon after the Genoese occupation.
Server Somuncuoğlu Sokağı.

Lala Mustafa Paşa Mosque (Cathedral of Agios Nikolaos)

It is remarkable that the Lusignans, so far from home, should have erected this large and formidable building. Construction work was started some time towards the end of the 13th century and may have taken 100 years to complete. The Lusignans must have been well satisfied with their achievement, for the cathedral is a fine example of French Gothic architecture. Their kings, already crowned in Nicosia, indulged themselves by being crowned 'Kings of Jerusalem' here.

The cathedral was considerably damaged during the siege of 1570, and soon after the conquest the Turks converted it into a mosque, adding the minaret that is so prominent today. The two great towers of the west front, once compared with those of Reims, lost part of their tops during the Ottoman siege. Despite everything, however, the west front remains a magnificent elevation with its three porches and the central six-light window. To each side are tall, walled-in windows surmounted by the windows of the damaged towers.

In the conversion to a mosque all images of the human form, whether in stone, fresco or stained glass, were removed in keeping with Islamic beliefs. It is likely that the porch niches housed statues of saints, and doubtless they were taken away at this time.

Today the interior is decorated simply and the floor covered with

Gazimağusa (Famagusta)

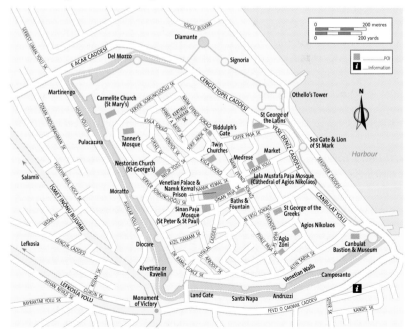

carpets. A few medieval tombs in the north aisle survived the conversion.
Naim Efendi Sokağı. Open: normally daily. Free admission except prayer times.

Medrese

This building was originally a medrese, a Muslim school for theological study. It was built by the Ottomans on the remains of a building from the Lusignan period. Today it is used as offices.
Liman Yolu Sokağı. Free admission.

Nestorian Church (St George's)

The Nestorians, or Chaldeans, came from Syria and the church was built for them in 1350 by a rich businessman called Francis Lakkas. Another name for the church is Agios Georgios Xorinos, meaning 'St George the Exiler'. It is claimed that dust from the floor of the church has the power to bring down one's enemies.
Off Somuncuoğlu Sokağı, by the Moratto Bastion.

Othello's Tower

Constructed in the 14th century, this distinctive citadel within the city walls carries the winged lion of St Mark, the badge of Venice, carved in stone above the entrance. Inside, the vaulted roof of the Great Hall, perhaps a refectory, is supported by Gothic arches. Steps lead to the battlements, and there are dramatic views over the city and the harbour. In earlier days the harbour

entrance was safeguarded by a huge chain hung from towers.

In Shakespeare's tragedy, Othello is sent to Cyprus to defend the Venetian port against an imminent Ottoman invasion.
In the ancient city walls, halfway along the east side on Cengiz Topel Caddesi. Open: Jun–Sept daily 10am–5pm; Oct–May daily 9am–1pm & 2–4.45pm. Admission charge.

Sinan Paşa Mosque (Church of St Peter and St Paul)

Built from 1358 to 1360, this Latin church is an adventurous structure of flying buttresses. With the takeover by the Ottomans in 1571 it was converted into a mosque.

During British rule it was used as a grain and potato store, and became known as the 'wheat mosque'. Some restoration work was carried out in 1961 and for a while the building was the city hall. Today it is the municipal library. In the yard is the tomb of Mehmet Efendi, a famous diplomat and literary figure of the 18th century who died in 1732.
Abdullah Paşa Sokağı. Closed to visitors.

St George of the Greeks

The large Church of St George may have been built in opposition to the Latin Cathedral of St Nicholas, for it was once the Orthodox cathedral. It is a dramatic ruin of conflicting styles. Most of it is Gothic but the decorated apses are in the Byzantine style. The

side of the church that faced the Canbulat Bastion took a terrific hammering in the siege of 1570, and it was probably at this time that the dome was destroyed.
Mustafa Ersu Sokağı.

St George of the Latins
The ruins suggest that this church must have been a splendid place. The lancet windows are tall and their sills set unusually high, perhaps for defensive purposes. It was built at the end of the 13th century and suffered damage during the siege of the town in 1570.
Cafer Paşa Sokağı, near Othello's Tower.

Tanner's Mosque
Originally a 16th-century church, the building was converted when the Ottoman Turks occupied Cyprus. Vases and earthenware bottles were used in the infill to the roof vaulting, as with other churches of this period.
Somuncuoğlu Sokağı.

Twin Churches of the Templars and Hospitallers
These two small 15th-century churches have been restored in recent times. They were built after the expulsion of the Templars and Hospitallers from Palestine in 1291.
Kışla Sokağı.

Venetian Palace and Namık Kemal Prison
Dating from the 13th century, the building was originally the royal palace of the Lusignans.

Earthquakes destroyed the main structure, leaving only the western

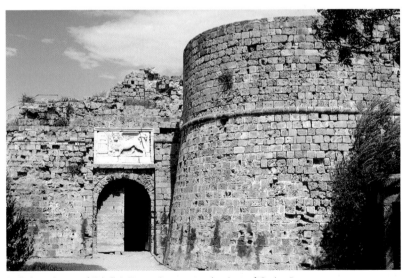

A climb to the top of Othello's Tower gives spectacular views of Gazimağusa

portion standing, although this is impressive enough. Three arches can be seen carried on columns that may well have come from Salamis. Over the central arch the keystone bears the coat of arms of Giovanni Renier, a Captain of Cyprus in 1552. It was here that Namık Kemal, a Turkish author and poet, was imprisoned after being deported from Istanbul in 1873. This part of the building now functions as a museum.

Sinan Paşa Sokağı. Open: Jun–Sept, Mon–Fri 9am–2pm; Oct–May, Mon–Fri 9am–1pm & 2–4.45pm. Closed: Sat & Sun. Free admission.

Venetian walls

Fifteen bastions are built into the 15m- (49ft-) high ramparts, which in some places are 8m (26ft) thick. There are five entrances, with the main **Land Gate** at the southwest corner of the rectangular enclosure. This gate lies adjacent to the original arched gateway and access to it is over a 19th-century bridge. Behind the gateway is the Ravelin, or Rivettina Bastion, housing a collection of guardrooms and dungeons. It was here in 1571 that the Turks first breached the walls and the surrender flag was hoisted. Within the gate there is a maze of passages connecting the gun chambers.

A ramp through the arch leads to the top of the Ravelin, opening on to a walk along the ramparts. Five more bastions are located along the southwest wall: the Diocare, Moratto,

THE SIEGE OF GAZIMAĞUSA

Gazimağusa was a fortified town long before the Venetians came to Cyprus. The increasing use of gunpowder in the Middle Ages had, however, completely changed the style of warfare. In 1490, the Venetians decided to remodel and strengthen the walls. Gun ports were built into them and the angular corners rounded off to deflect cannonballs. Gazimağusa became one of the strongest fortified cities in the Middle East.

Even so, the efforts of the Venetians in the end proved to be of no avail. The Ottomans broke through in 1571. Nevertheless, it had taken ten months of terrible siege tactics and the death of 50,000 Turkish soldiers as against 6,000 Venetians and Greeks. The Venetian commander Marco Antonio Bragadin was obliged to meet with the Turk Mustafa Paşa, who had him flayed alive and his skin stuffed and paraded around the town.

Pulacazara and San Luca bastions, with the last in line, Martinengo Bastion, collecting the adjacent walls into a huge spearhead plan form, which proved impregnable to the Turks. The walls are 6m (20ft) thick in places. Here, the angular corners were not rounded off, and double cannon ports were built into the walls.

The north wall was defended by the Del Mozzo and Diamante bastions. Turning seawards the small Signoria Bastion is passed and the famous citadel, or Othello's Tower, is reached. To the south of the tower is the Sea Gate (Porta del Mare), complete with the remains of an iron portcullis and iron-clad doors built by the Ottoman Turks. In Venetian times the sea came right up to the gate. The stone lion is not another badge of Venice; more probably it is a simple medieval sculpture.

From this point, a long stretch of wall extends to the Canbulat or Arsenal Gate and Bastion in the city's southeast corner. It is here that the Turkish General Canbulat Bey died in the siege. It seems he committed a great suicidal act of bravery, which opened the way for his men to enter the gate. For this he was declared a martyr and buried within the bastion, a tomb being erected over his resting place, which is now a place of pilgrimage for Turks. The precincts leading off the gate were converted to a museum in 1968.

The Turks made vigorous attempts to breach the defences of this gate, and until recently the area was a treasure trove of cannonballs and bits of metal. From here to the Land Gate, the bastions of Camposanto, Andruzzi and Santa Napa punctuate the southern wall. Caution should be taken on the wall for there are many unguarded openings and dangerous drops.

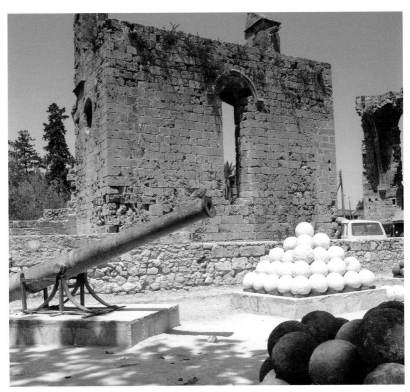

The ruins of the Venetian Palace

Life in the north

Northern Cyprus, within sight of the shores of modern-day Turkey, is unmistakably Eastern. The muezzin calls the faithful to prayer, although it may well be that the mosque was a Christian church many centuries before. However, the Turkish Cypriots today are not fervent about their religion. Their language is, of course, Turkish, although not the purer form, for it is a local dialect.

Life has an easy pace; it may even have slipped back a little in time since the turmoil of 1974. Certainly there is only occasional evidence of the frenetic holiday activity that characterises the rest of the island.

Nevertheless, tourism is an important foreign currency earner. Agriculture is another, with citrus, vegetable and grain production being of greatest importance. In the towns

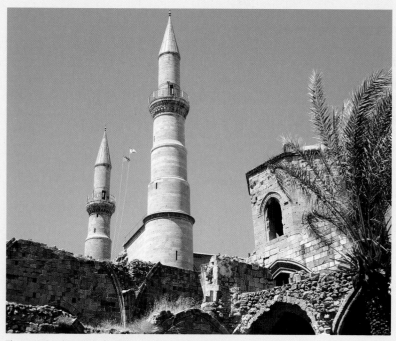

The towering minarets of Lefkoşa's Selimiye Mosque

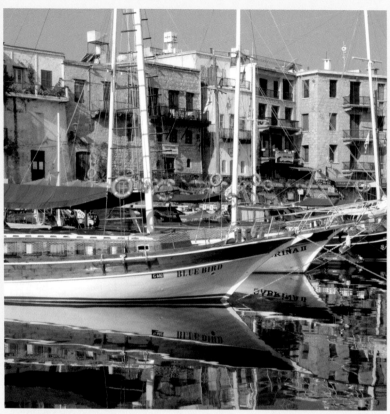

Boats moored in Girne

people shop in bazaars. Hand-carts stacked high with fresh fruit go rolling along the narrow streets, and if two should meet, then the way is blocked for minutes while the vendors convey the traditional greetings.

On a national holiday the village coffee shops will be more crowded than usual. The all-male clientele will sit and gossip. The rules and courtesies of hospitality, so much a part of life in the Middle East, are not to be waived. A Turkish coffee will be offered (there is no ambiguity here about its name as there is in the south) and it must be accepted. The same applies to the strong Turkish cigarette proffered with it. Little English is spoken in the villages but the gestures come thick and fast, and the interpreter will have to work overtime to keep up.

GAZIMAĞUSA ENVIRONS
Apostolos Varnavas

The monastery was built in honour of the apostle when a sepulchre containing his remains and a copy of the Gospel of Matthew in Barnabas's handwriting were found on the site in AD 478.

Nothing remains of the original structure apart from a foundation and a marble column. Much of the destruction is attributed to Arab raiders. The present building was erected in the 18th century. Inside are life-size frescoes painted in recent times, depicting scenes of the granting of independence to the Church of Cyprus in AD 431.

A custodian will show people round the church.

13km (8 miles) northwest of Gazimağusa. Open: Tue–Sat. Admission charge.

Egkomi

The ruins of this late Bronze Age city lie on the north bank of the Pediaios River.

This extensive collection of holes in the ground is of great significance to the archaeological history of Cyprus. The earliest remains date from the 17th century BC and suggest that the city was once the capital of Cyprus. It prospered through the export of copper and trade with Syria. In the 16th century BC Mycenaean craftsmen came to the city to produce vases and a ceramic industry evolved. Three hundred years later there was an influx of Achaean settlers.

Unfortunately, much of the city was destroyed by a great fire, and subsequent earthquakes in the 12th century BC levelled much of what remained. Recovery was impossible and within 100 years Egkomi was abandoned, the people moving to nearby Salamis.

Originally the site was considered to be no more than a necropolis; then in 1896, a British Museum expedition discovered a number of tombs containing gold, ivory and pottery of

The remains of Kantara Castle's northeast tower

the Mycenaean period. Later discoveries included a now-famous clay tablet of Cypro-Minoan script and, in 1950, the Horned God of the 12th century BC, a priceless bronze figure now in the Cyprus Museum (*see pp28–30*).

Visitors should start at the North Gate and proceed south to visit the **Sanctuary of the Horned God**, followed by **building 18**, the **House of the Pillar** and the **House of the Bronzes**. The latter is the remains of a 12th-century BC stone building found piled high with bronze objects.

10km (6 miles) northwest of Gazimağusa. Open: Jun–Sept daily 9am–7pm; Oct–May daily 9am–1pm & 2–4.45pm. Admission charge.

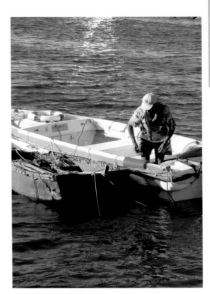

A fisherman off the Karpaz Yarımadası (Karpasia) Peninsula

Kantara Castle

The castle's origins rest in Byzantine times, but it was the Lusignans who built the great ramparts, to complete Cyprus's northern chain of defences. Its stature is less than that of its sisters, Voufavento and Agios Ilarion, but it is no less splendid for that. The castle dominates the northern shore and looks out over the Karpasia Peninsula towards Turkey. To the south is the magnificent sweep of scenic Gazimağusa Bay.

Much of the interior lies in ruins but the formidable outer wall is practically intact. Entrance is gained through a ruined barbican with twin towers, followed by a climb up some steps to reach a vaulted room. Opposite is the southeast tower with its vaulted guard quarters and cistern below. By proceeding along the south wall a tour in a clockwise direction is commenced. On the left is a barracks, complete with slit windows, and a latrine showing the vestiges of a complex flushing system. More ruined chambers are passed as the path leads on to the final ascent. A room with Gothic windows marks the highest vantage point.

4km (2¹/₂ miles) northeast of Kantara village, 38km (24 miles) north of Gazimağusa. Open: Jun–Sept daily 10am–5pm; Oct–May daily 9am–1pm & 2–4.45pm. Free admission.

Karpaz Yarımadası (Karpasia) Peninsula

Also known as the 'Panhandle', this distinctive land formation has ancient ruins and secluded beaches hidden

along its unspoilt shores. At the very eastern extremity is the monastery of Apostolos Andreas, and there are several splendid Byzantine churches on the Karpaz.
Northeast Cyprus.

Salamis

This is the most impressive and important archaeological site in Cyprus. The ruins are in two distinct sections separated by the main road. To the west is a necropolis with several intriguing tombs; to the east the ancient city itself. Three groups of ruins can be identified. Close to the main road are the Roman *agora* and the Temple of Zeus. Over on the east are the Kampanopetra and the ancient harbour. To the north are the gymnasium, baths and theatre. It is from the gymnasium area that the tour described below commences. It should be appreciated that the distance from the gymnasium to the Temple of Zeus is no less than 900m (½ mile).

The columns of the **gymnasium** are plainly visible. Many are from the nearby theatre, having been transferred during the Byzantine reconstruction of Salamis. These columns were re-erected in the 1950s.

From here we reach the main building of the baths, the *caldarium*, where the water was heated from underground furnaces off the adjoining north hall. Some restored mosaics can be seen in the south hall. Ninety metres (300ft) to the south is the impressive

THE CITY OF SALAMIS

Salamis was a city kingdom, its exact date of origin unknown. However, various artefacts discovered on the site date from the 11th century BC. Salamis rapidly became the most influential of the kingdoms of Cyprus and remained so for over 1,000 years.

The kings of Salamis resisted the encroachments of the Persians and then the Ptolemies of Egypt. They were only partially successful in their defence but Salamis still continued as an important commercial centre under the Romans, although severe earthquakes in AD 76 and AD 77 caused much damage. Again in the 4th century, earthquakes and tidal waves left Salamis in ruins. A new city was then commissioned, which survived until the 7th century. The city lay beneath the sands for centuries and it was not until 1880 that the first excavations took place.

Roman theatre, discovered in 1959. Most of what can be seen has been reconstructed. It was probably built at the end of the 1st century AD, only to be destroyed by earthquakes during the 4th century.

Continuing south, the remains of a **Roman villa** are passed, and turning left along the road, a **Byzantine cistern** is found. Inside are paintings and inscriptions. Further south is the **Kampanopetra**, a large early Christian basilica, only partially excavated. The **ancient harbour** is a few hundred metres ahead.

Beyond the crossroads is the **Granite Forum**, where columns of impressive dimensions lie on the site. A little further to the south are the barely discernible remains of a second, 4th-century basilica, **Agios Epifanios**.

If the road is followed round to the right the *vouta* is reached. This is a 7th-century cistern, or reservoir, that received water from Kythrea, 56km (35 miles) away, via an aqueduct. Close by is the *agora*, dating from the times of Caesar Augustus and measuring 230m by 55m (755ft by 180ft).

At the far end, a few unimpressive stones are all that remain today to mark the site of the **Temple of Zeus.** From here it is a short distance to the main road and then on to the western half of the site. A few hundred metres along the road is the **Royal Necropolis.** Several tombs can be found, described mainly by numbers, although some have names.

By the side of the road is tomb 50, **St Catherine's Prison**, built in Roman times but standing above the 7th-century BC tombs. Others worth seeking out are numbers **47** and **49**, both having skeletons of horses which have been cast in the concrete floor.

10km (6 miles) north of Gazimağusa. Open: Apr–Oct daily 9am–7pm; Nov–Mar daily 9am–1pm & 2–4.45pm. Admission charge.

Salamis

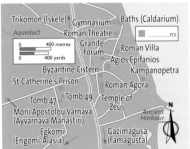

The columns of the Salamis gymnasium

GIRNE (KYRENIA)
Decorative Arts Museum
The museum exhibits oil paintings, handicrafts from the Far East, and European and Chinese porcelain.

Paşabahçe Sokağı. Open: Jun–Sept daily 9am–7pm; Oct–May daily 9am–1pm & 2–4.45pm. Admission charge.

Folk Art Museum
The building itself is a model of an 18th-century Greek-Cypriot house. Various handmade objects, pieces of 18th-century furniture and the implements used to make them are displayed.

By the harbour. Open: Jun–Sept daily 9am–2pm; Oct–May daily 9am–1pm & 2–4.45pm. Admission charge.

Girne Castle

A castle has stood on this waterfront site for centuries. Certainly the Byzantines built a fort, maybe as long ago as the 7th century. The Lusignans extended it and then the Venetians remodelled it, creating what we see today. The huge cylindrical bastion that pushes out into the harbour is their work and is fully intact.

Lusignan kings regularly stayed in the castle to shelter or rest, and it was here that Eleanor of Aragon, the jealous wife of Peter I, had his mistress Jeanne Laleman imprisoned.

In more recent times it was used as a prison by the British until it became the responsibility of the Directorate of Antiquities and Museums.

From the entrance, the main route leads directly from the gatehouse to the main courtyard, passing a narrow passage leading to a 12th-century Byzantine chapel.

The northwest tower should be examined before proceeding to the courtyard. Here, at the entrance, is the tomb of Sadik Paşa, the Turkish admiral to whom the castle was surrendered in 1570 by the Venetians. The **Shipwreck Museum** is found on the east side and contains the priceless Kyrenia ship. Across the courtyard to the west are the royal apartments, although unfortunately they are not very well preserved. Below are dungeons.

The battlements are accessible from the northwest tower. Walking

Girne (Kyrenia)

along the walls requires care as there are unguarded drops. From the north wall the eastern ramparts can be reached, or a descent made through various chambers to the courtyard.

The southwest tower (Venetian) is entered from the battlements. A passage leads down to the angular bastion and along the west wall, back to the courtyard entrance.

The waterfront. Open: Jun–Sept daily 9am–7pm; Oct–May daily 9am–1pm & 2–4.45pm. Admission charge.

Girne Ship

This is one of the oldest vessels ever to be recovered from the sea. It was wrecked around 300 BC in shallow waters, less than 1.5km (1 mile) from the anchorage of Kyrenia.

The wreck was lifted during the summers of 1968 and 1969 by a team from the University of Pennsylvania. So delicate was the work that it was another six years before it was reassembled. The wooden hull was made of Aleppo pine and measured 14m

(46ft) long by 4.5m (15ft) across, and carried a single sail. The ship could make 4½ knots and when it sank it was already about 80 years old. The cargo consisted of more than 400 wine amphorae from Rhodes, jars of almonds, and 29 millstones. To keep the timber in good condition the atmosphere of the museum is strictly controlled.

Girne Castle. Open: castle hours. Admission charge included in the ticket for the castle.

Icon Museum

This museum is housed in a church dedicated to the Archangel Michael, and contains the church's original iconostasis in carved wood and over 40 paintings of various periods from churches in the area.

In the tower of the Archangel Michael Church, western end of the harbour. Open: Jun–Sept daily 9am–7pm; Oct–May daily 9am–1pm & 2–4.45pm.

Lusignan Towers

Girne was once a walled town, fortified by the Lusignans against attack from land and sea. Some of the towers built into the wall have survived. There is one by the harbour and the foundations of another by the customs house. The most intact of the towers is on Hürriyet Caddesi near the market.

The fortified harbour at Girne

GIRNE ENVIRONS
Acheiropoietos Monastery

Since its foundation in the 12th century this monastery has undergone many alterations, being rebuilt in the 14th century and later acquiring a large apse. *By the sea on Acheiropoietos Point, north of Karavas (see also Lambusa, p133).*

Agios Ilarion (St Hilarion)

The castle may have been named after St Hilarion the Great, the founder of monasticism in Palestine, or a later St Hilarion from the Holy Land. Whatever the truth, the Byzantines built a church here in the 10th century in memory of a St Hilarion. It developed into a monastery and soon became fortified.

During the Lusignan reign the fortifications were strengthened with the construction of strong outer walls. After the occupation of Cyprus by the Venetians in 1489, however, the new administration ordered the dismantling of St Hilarion along with Voufavento and Kantara castles.

Once through the entrance, the visitor will see a restored gatehouse and, on the left, a barbican. By the south wall is a cistern, and, further on, the stables. An ascent to the next level brings some fine views of the walls and a semicircular tower. From this position the middle ward is entered to reach the 10th-century Byzantine church at the top of the stairs.

Bellapaïs Abbey, nestling among the lower slopes of the hills around Girne

Steps descend to a vaulted passage and a hall that may have been a refectory; the passage leads on to a belvedere with adjacent kitchens. The accommodation to the northeast was for the royal family. Today, this is a café. The upper ward is a separate entity, reached by a path from the middle ward.

At a good height an ascent to the left of the main route leads to St John's Tower, sheer on three sides, from where a prince of Antioch hurled his enemies.

Regaining the main route, paths and steps lead on through an arched gateway. The Queen's Window has side seats and although it has lost much of its tracery, it retains a marvellous view. *8km (5 miles) southwest of Girne. Open: Jun–Sept daily 9am–5pm; Oct–May daily 9am–1pm & 2–4.45pm. Admission charge.*

Agios Mamas (St Mammes Church and Icon Museum)

The church and monastery is in the sizeable town of Güzelyurt, a tortuous maze of narrow streets and alleys. It was founded in Byzantine times but nothing remains from this period. Extensive rebuilding was carried out in the 15th century, some of which still survives. However, a substantial portion of the present construction was added during the 18th century. Inside the church the iconostasis is of various styles; the lower panels display fine Venetian craftsmanship. A recess in the north wall is the very impressive tomb of St Mammes himself.

Access is by courtesy of the custodian of the small **Museum of Nature and Archaeology** next door, which contains bronze artefacts, Hellenistic pottery and a 4,000-year-old statue. *Güzelyurt, 37km (23 miles) west of Lefkosia. Museum. Open: Jun–Sept daily 9am–7pm; Oct–May daily 9am–4.45pm. Admission charge.*

Alevkaya Herbarium

Established in 1989 by the Forestry Department, this is a collection of some 900 plant specimens, many of which are indigenous to the Beşparmak Mountains. *22km (14 miles) east of Girne, on the road to Değirmenlik (Kythrea). Open: daily 9am–5pm.*

Antifonitis Church

The outside looks a little neglected, but this church is substantially as it used to be before the Turkish Cypriots took over northern Cyprus in 1974. From the central octagonal plan a dome of red tiles is carried on four columns and four piers. To the south, the 15th-century veranda is in disrepair. *29km (18 miles) east of Girne, via the track from Esentepe. Open: Jun–Sept daily 9am–2pm; Oct–May daily 9am–1pm & 2–4.45pm.*

Bellapaïs Abbey

The precise origins of the abbey in the village of Beylerbeyi are not clear, but it is known that it was founded in the 13th century by Augustinian canons.

Free-standing arches remain from an arcade in the Bellapaïs Abbey

The Latin kings of Cyprus supported the canons and Hugh III went as far as bestowing upon the abbot the privilege of wearing the mitre and golden spurs. The good times came to a sudden end in 1570 when the Ottomans destroyed much of the complex. The abbey deteriorated, and not until 1912 were serious attempts made at restoration.

In the forecourt is the church, the earliest surviving part of the complex. Access is not usually offered by the custodian but may be on request. The interior is a Frankish Gothic design with a nave, two aisles, a north and south transept and chancel. Access to the dormitory is by a night stair, and, to the west, a spiral stair continues to the roof providing a magnificent view of the Beşparmak Mountains. Back in the forecourt a doorway leads to the centrepiece of Bellapaïs, the cloister with its tall dark cypress trees. Although a ruin, with the arches of the arcade to the west having lost their vaults, it is an impressive place with fine Gothic detailing.

In the northwest corner lies a large marble sarcophagus and lavabo where monks washed their hands before entering the refectory. This splendid vaulted hall is unequalled in Cyprus. On the east side is a rose window, and a staircase within the thickness of one wall rises up to the pulpit. Six windows in the north wall reveal a magnificent view over the coast.

East of the cloister is the chapter house and an undercroft, complete with the stone benches used by the canons. On the same level is a vaulted treasury.

6.5km (4 miles) southeast of Girne. Open: Jun–mid-Sept daily 9am–7pm; mid-Sept–May daily 9am–1pm & 2–4.45pm. Admission charge.

Bufavento (Voufavento) Castle

This is not the best preserved of the three great elevated castles of the northern mountains, but at 790m (2,590ft) above sea level it is the highest.

During the winter months the cold Anatolian wind can blow, a sharp reminder that the Italian name of the castle means 'blown by the wind'. Not much is known of the castle's history, but it certainly existed in the 12th century. A garrison was in occupation until well into the Venetian period, but ironically, the last few years of this foreign domination saw the castle dismantled and left to the elements.

From the remains of the gatehouse a long flight of worn steps leads up the high crag, passing the chambers of the lower ward, which was constructed over a vaulted water system. Further steps lead to the upper ward and the remains

of a chapel. The visitor can go no further, for all around the land falls away and the view is breathtaking, leaving no doubts as to why the Lusignans chose such a site.

13km (8 miles) southeast of Girne. The approach is from the east, along the rough track from the high pass of the Beşparmak Mountains. Cars should be left in the car park. From there it is a 4km (2½-mile) walk.

Lambusa (Lampousa)

Over the years this site has been occupied by Greeks, Phoenicians, Ptolemies, Romans and Byzantines, as well as being one of the Hittite or city kingdoms of Cyprus. In pre-Christian times Lambusa was a major exporter of pottery. Little remains today, although the Roman fish tanks with their inlet and outlet channels have survived, and the supports to their sluice gates are still in position. In the early 20th century the Lambusa Treasure, including several silver plates from the 7th century, was unearthed. Much of it is preserved in the Cyprus Museum (*see pp28–30*).

On the shore, west of Girne, 1.5km (1 mile) from Karavas (see also Acheiropoietos Monastery, p130).

Lefke (Lefka)

This town has been inhabited by Turkish Cypriots for more than 400 years, and has an authentic Turkish-Cypriot atmosphere.

52km (32 miles) west of Lefkosia.

Soloi

The city was founded at the beginning of the 6th century BC and took its name in honour of Solon, the Athenian statesman who came to Cyprus in his old age. It prospered and became one of the ten city kingdoms of Cyprus, playing an important role in the struggle against Persian domination. Nearby were the copper mines of Skouriotissa and Mavrovouni, and with the arrival of the Romans, Cyprus became a major copper exporter.

The Romans constructed the **theatre** on the hillside, possibly on the site of a smaller Greek one. Some 3,500 seats were built into the hillside, overlooking the sea. It was discovered in 1930 and subsequently restored. Much of the original stonework had been removed in the 18th century, some being used in the building of the Suez Canal. Only the floor of the orchestra and stage area is the original.

Lower down the hill is the **basilica**, built in the 5th century, and abandoned after Arab raids in AD 632. A small part of the mosaic floor has survived and the bird designs are of special interest. Over to the west is the *agora*, very little of which has survived.

It was at Soloi that the famous marble statue of Aphrodite was found, now kept in the Cyprus Museum. To the west and just offshore is the island rock of Limnitis. During the excavations at Soloi, the Swedish archaeologists visited the island and discovered various pieces of pottery and tools from the Neolithic period.

The southern shore of Güzelyurt Bay, 20km (12½ miles) southwest of Güzelyurt. Open: Jun–Sept daily 9am–7pm; Oct–May daily 9am–1pm & 2–4.45pm. Admission charge.

Vuni (Vouni Palace)

The site is breathtaking, overlooking the sea from a high plateau. Inland the panorama is almost as spectacular.

Excavations were first carried out between 1928 and 1929. Nothing earlier than the 5th century BC was uncovered, making the palace more recent than anticipated. Nevertheless, there is good evidence that it was built by a pro-Persian king when parts of the island were in unsuccessful revolt against the Persians. The palace would serve to hold in check nearby Soloi, which had sided with the rebels. Other evidence suggests the palace is of later origins, perhaps built after the revolt which set a pro-Greek dynasty in power around 498 BC. We may never know the true story of Vuni's origins but it had a brief existence, being set alight in 380 BC, when the Persians regained control of Cyprus.

Little remains of the walls, but it seems clear that there were several different distinct periods of construction. The main entrance of the palace is approached from the southwest and passes into the megaron and royal apartments. Down a few steps is a peristyle court with surrounding rooms. In the centre of the court is a cistern, and, by the wellhead, a stone slab that would at one time have carried a windlass.

The water system of the palace was quite elaborate and designed to supply all the major rooms. Well-arranged baths were served by this complex plumbing and had a ready supply of hot and cold water. Some distance from the palace are various shrines, and several interesting sculptures have been found close by. To the south, up on the high ground, is what little remains of the **Temple of Athena**.

South of Güzelyurt Bay, 27km (17 miles) west of Güzelyurt.
Open: Jun–Sept daily 10am–5pm; Oct–May daily 9am–1pm & 2–4.45pm. Admission charge.

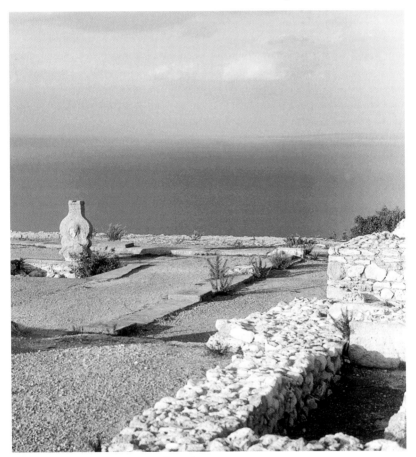

The remains of Vuni occupy a spectacular setting

Getting away from it all

Famed for the sapphire-coloured seas that surround this little island, Cyprus offers more than just beaches and cruises. Lesser-known mountain trails, for the more hardy and adventurous, abound, while forests and waterfalls create havens of cool and comfort for the less intrepid traveller. A sense of history prevails wherever you go – from the more frequented south to the remote end of the Karpaz Peninsula in the extreme northeast.

SOUTHERN CYPRUS
Akra Pomou (Pomos) to Kato Pyrgos

The beaches on this stretch of coast, east of Chrysochou Bay in western Cyprus, are still pristine and quiet. There are several good stretches of sand and pretty fishing harbours with boats bobbing. The views of the coast from above the Turkish enclave of Erenköy (Kokkina) are spectacular. Here the mountain air is fresh, the pine forest is beautiful, and you'll share the road with herds of goats. Take it slowly.

Down again on the coast, the road eventually reaches Kato Pyrgos. The village is of no great merit but provides a fine lunchtime stop. It is, of course, literally the end of the line, being the western extremity of the military division of Cyprus, but there is a border crossing here to the north.

Akrotirio (Cape) Arnaoutis

Geographically, the cape of western Cyprus is as remote as anywhere on the island, with a road that peters out some 9km (5¹/₂ miles) to the east. Therefore, most explorers of this stretch of coast might expect to have it to themselves. The fact that this is not the case is attributable to one thing – the motorbike. Many of today's visitors to Cyprus have the skill, even with a pillion passenger, to traverse the bumpy track, with ruts deeper than can be imagined, from the Baths of Aphrodite to the cape.

So, perhaps not unreasonably, one has to share this magnificent territory with a few others. And, of course, now there is a choice of how the visitor can get there. One can join the 'bikers' and risk the bumps and a possible plummet into the sea from a great height, or make enquiries to share or hire a 4WD vehicle. Walking there and back (18km/11 miles) will not appeal to everybody, and would be more than an exhausting punishment in summer. The answer for foot travellers is to go to Latchi and find a boatman willing to

Lacemaking is a common sight in villages

On leaving the cape, walkers have to decide between the easy inland track or the shore, the ground in between being a mass of impenetrable bushes. It is a fascinating landscape: the rocks are white, the soil deep red, and the sea a tempting blue. To the south, a church stands silhouetted on the hills of the Akamas. A detour through the bush might disturb a hare, but only a silver flash will be seen. Twenty minutes after leaving the cape, two coastal wrecks will be reached. They appear to have met their unfortunate end some time ago and now provide a refuge for countless species of marine life.

Although the cape is now behind, the panorama ahead more than makes up for it. The shoreline is never less than wonderful and the unusual flat-topped hill of **Vakhines** stands magnificent in the middle distance. Now is perhaps the time to seek out a secluded cove and try the cool waters. There is, however, no hurry, for it is more or less the same all the way to distant Agios Georgios Island. Certainly the land turns from red to white and one may be passed by a bike or two, or a truck full of goats, but things are hardly the worse for this.

It comes as something of a surprise to realise that this part of the Akamas is popular with local hunters and was once a British Army firing range. Large red signs warn walkers to keep well away from the red flags and not to touch objects on the ground as 'they may explode and kill you'!

take them to the cape or partway along the peninsula, then hike back. It is essential to leave the car at the Baths of Aphrodite and be picked up from the beach there, otherwise the walking is extended by 4.5km (2³/4 miles). Speedboats do the trip in 20 minutes, and the costs can be reduced by sharing with another party. Boat travellers should be aware that disembarkation can involve a leap and a splash.

Specific destinations are irrelevant in this wonderful area. The cape itself is fine enough, but, low-lying and rocky, it is no place for a swim, although an ideal spot for a picnic. A little to the east, some shelves in the rock seem ideal for sunbathing. Around the cape to the south are dramatic-looking sea cliffs, though sufficiently distant to discourage thoughts of exploration.

The long march to Loutra Afroditis
(Baths of Aphrodite) allows time to
ponder on the fate of this unique
part of Cyprus.

Camel trail

The trail runs from the high Troodos
Mountains to the port of Pafos. To
follow it along its length is rather an
ambitious temptation. However, to
meet up with it for half a day is still
quite an experience.

The Venetians cut the route through
the hills to improve trade and
communications. Initially, copper
from the Troodos mines was the
main commodity.

Three rivers barred the way: a
tributary of the Diarizos, the Diarizos
itself, and the Xeros. This was not a
problem to such master builders as the
Venetians and they bridged them all.
Elea Bridge is the furthest east, Kelephos
is in the middle, and Roudhias at the
western end where the route starts to
descend towards the coast.

The trail is unused today, although a
dirt road approximates to it and carries
the occasional vehicle. This suggested
trip starts in the west at the village of
Galataria. For safety and comfort a
4WD vehicle is required, ground
clearance being an important factor.
A plentiful supply of water and fuel

The trails of the Troodos Mountains are loved by serious trekkers

should be carried. Locals, however, swear the best way to do it is on horseback, foot or mountain bike.

From the village take the road to Koilineia and the start of the stony, but tolerable, road to the deserted village of Vretsia, 4km (2¹/2 miles) away. On nearing the centre, with its little memorial, the reason for the abandonment becomes quite clear, explained in an instant by the mosque and its battered minaret. This is a Turkish village and everybody left in 1974.

The way out of any Cypriot village is perplexing, and escape from a deserted one borders on the impossible. At the time of printing, the best choice of exit was to turn right at the memorial through some houses, down an atrocious road which, thankfully, quickly improves. A track to the right, leading to more buildings, should be ignored, and soon after leaving the village, take the next fork to the right. It is another 5km (3 miles) to the bridge, which can be seen in the valley after about 4km (2¹/2 miles).

This is a convenient place to stop and climb out on to the hillside. On a calm day the silence is as nowhere else, eerie, almost disturbing. There are no tourist motorbikes, just the marvellous view over the valley to great white cliffs, and the silence. In midsummer, the heat on this southern slope is murderous; it is no place to break down or get stuck. Drivers should make no move forward if they feel they may not be able to reverse out of it. However, on the correct track, with common sense, there should be little trouble. In spring and autumn, it may be a worthwhile idea to park and walk down to the bridge; in summer, driving is the sensible choice.

Once by the bridge, an immediate difficulty presents itself. A cursory examination of the Venetian edifice indicates that a laden camel would have the hardest of times crossing it. However, there are more pressing matters. What is much more important is to put on a pair of flip-flops and wander down the Xeros River through the trees. In spring there may be too much water for this; in the summer, there will be only a little. Within 250m (275yds), a series of pools will be reached which have the clearest, purest and coolest water imaginable. Not a second should be lost in taking the plunge, and if nothing else does, this will make the whole trip to Cyprus worthwhile. Once fully restored, with a body temperature approaching normal, it will be easier to explore the river bed and its surrounding area. Intrepid visitors may wish to continue along the camel route to Gafyra Kelephou (Kelephos Bridge), or even as far as Elea Bridge.

On a cautionary note, keep an eye open for snakes, and avoid the river bed if a thunderstorm is raging up the valley in the Troodos.

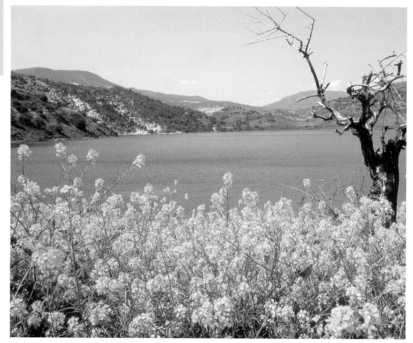

The lake at Germasogeia Dam, near Lemesos

Cruises from Larnaka

There are boat trips to Larnaka Bay and Agia Napa from the marina area and the small harbour at the south end of the town. Agia Napa is no less than 37km (23 miles) distant, a long way, and requiring precautions against sunburn.

Cruises to Kolpos Lara (Lara Bay) Beach

The beach is no longer undiscovered, but a visit from Pafos is still a wonderful day out for those who enjoy boat trips in the sun. At 25km (15½ miles), the trip is a long one and precautions should be taken against sunburn. There are two beaches (*see p91*), one on either side of the headland, where the splendour of the sand and sea matches the views of the Akamas Hills. A turtle hatchery protects the endangered loggerhead turtles in the natural habitat.

Cyprus's dams

Cyprus has several picturesque dams, some of which are splendid places to stop for a picnic. The dam above Germasogeia, near Lemesos, is a renowned favourite. Another, east of Pafos by the village of Foinikas, is twice as big, and picnic and birdwatching possibilities exist on numerous stretches of the bank.

Evretou Dam, off the Pafos–Polis road near Skoulli, is another recent development, and is well worth the 2km (1¼-mile) detour off the main road.

Ghost city of Varosha

There are cruises from the harbour of Agia Napa that pass around Cape Gkreko to Fig Tree Bay and head up the coast to stand off and peer at the derelict and abandoned beachside development of Varosha, a suburb of Gazimağusa, stranded in no-man's-land since the 1974 invasion.

Those who want to see the city can drive to Deryneia and then go to a private viewing platform (well signposted) to see the deserted town through telescopes and binoculars.

Koilada tou Kedron (Cedar Valley)

Despite much publicity, this valley in the western Troodos is not overrun with tourists. Few people set out for the valley and even fewer get there. An explanation is its isolation and a twisting and turning sealed road leading to it.

In reality, a visit to Cedar Valley is the high spot of a trip through the cool western forest.

The cedars, mainly the *Cedrus Libani* from Lebanon, grow to a great height. They flourish at altitudes ranging from 1,000 to 1,400m (3,281–4,593ft).

The road, while narrow and winding, is excellent, and is very well signposted. Indeed, there is now a superb network of sealed roads criss-crossing the Troodos.

Lush Cedar Valley in the Troodos Mountains, a paradise off the beaten track

Admiring the beauty of the Cypriot coastline from a cruise boat

Papoutsa

Papoutsa's height of 1,562m (5,125ft) above sea level in the eastern Troodos is more than respectable and no roads run to its rocky summit. Olympos does its best to block out the view to the west, but even so, the panorama is amazing. Cars can be left on the high pass where the road from Palekhori to Agios Theodhoros is met by the one from Agros. Papoutsa is the peak to the southeast, the ridge of which runs right down to the pass.

The ascent does not entail hours of footslogging. The hill can be rushed in 25 minutes or taken more leisurely in 45. The ridge is easy walking, although every step is uphill. There are some fine specimens of dried flowers – dead but still in the ground – on these heights. The summit is something of a surprise; a large cross and a stone shelter are more reminiscent of northern European hills than Cyprus.

Wine villages

Cyprus has some superb wines, some of the best coming from Marathasa, Pitsilia, Solea and Tilliria. It is the

Krassochoria (the wine villages), found in the southwest Troodos, 32km (20 miles) from Lemesos that are most interesting.

The main villages are **Omodos**, **Pachna** and **Arsos**. They are not too far apart and all can be reached by roads. Old traditions have survived where cultivation of the vineyards and winemaking are still the main occupation of most of the inhabitants. The product of their efforts is a dry red wine. In Omodos, an old farmhouse has been restored, complete with wine press. The village itself has been specially renovated for tourism.

NORTHERN CYPRUS
Beşparmak Mountains (Pentadaktylos)

The Greek name Pentadaktylos means 'five fingers', and, indeed, Beşparmak mountain itself has five unusual spiky summits. Cars could be left at the top of the pass, 16km (10 miles) southeast of Girne, where a path runs along the south face and from which the rocky peaks are plainly visible. One can simply admire the features of the ridge from here and watch the griffon vultures alighting on the inaccessible pinnacles, or climb the lower slopes until the going gets hard. The place is teeming with vipers, so care is needed where feet and hands are placed.

Güzelyurt Bay (Morfou Bay)

There is approximately 40km (25 miles) of this attractive western shore, much of it sandy. Access is through Güzelyurt itself and then through Yayla.

Another possibility for exploring is further to the north via Akdeniz and on to the shore by the Bronze Age site of **Paleokastro**. It is found on a hill overlooking the sea. An intriguing collection of over 2,000 earthenware male figures discovered here is now in the Cyprus Museum in Lefkosia (*see pp28–30*).

Karpaz Yarımadası (Karpasia)

The one sure place to get away from it all in Cyprus is the Karpaz Peninsula, for it is a long way from the main cities. It is an unusual land formation, nearly 80km (50 miles) long and 11km (7 miles) wide. From Lefkosia or Girne, it's only a couple of hours along an attractive road to the start of the peninsula. Gazimağusa is also a good starting point.

The road runs along the coast with occasional roads and tracks that take you even closer to the sea. There are ancient sites on both shores. **Galunya** (**Galounia**) is the first on the north side, and perhaps this was the town of ancient Aphrodision.

There are several small bays and inlets along the coast until Cape Apostolos Andreas, where the ancient site of **Kastros** is reached together with the journey's end.

On the south side of the peninsula, the rocky shore occasionally gives way to sandy dunes, spectacular beaches and a shallow sea.

Shopping

Cyprus is not exactly the shopping capital of Europe, but in the last couple of years shopping malls have opened in most of the major towns, offering a much wider choice of purchases than previously. If you're looking for souvenirs, it's best to go for locally made goods such as pottery, jewellery, basketware, lace and embroidery, but there are plenty of shops in the tourist resorts that offer everything from luminous sunglasses to T-shirts with dubious slogans.

An oddity which might not immediately spring to mind as a holiday purchase is spectacles. There are many qualified opticians in Cyprus and they can supply glasses within 24 hours at much cheaper prices than at home. Many now offer a special tourist service.

SOUTHERN CYPRUS
Greek-Cypriot Lefkosia
Ledra and Onasagorou
These two narrow pedestrianised streets are the focus of the old town. There are many stylish boutiques and shoe shops catering mainly for local trade, but visitors may be able to pick up bargains. The shops are the typical high-street stores and global franchises found in most European capitals, with the occasional store selling local products such as lace or icons.

Laiki Geitonia
Laiki Geitonia is a restored district which tries to evoke the atmosphere of old Lefkosia. There are many tourist shops, some of which sell better-than-average souvenirs. Try here for jewellery, cloth, rugs and pottery.

There are several places to buy leather goods, including shoes, handbags and suitcases. The area is particularly pleasant to walk around, and there are plenty of cafés and restaurants at which to rest and watch the world go by.

The new town and Archbishop Makarios III Avenue
This broad avenue has a completely different ambience. This is where the locals shop and the stores are very chic. There are plenty of expensive boutiques, shoe and jewellery shops, as well as sports retailers. There are two modern shopping plazas, many 'high-end' boutiques and hip cafés. This is Lefkosia's busiest shopping street; it is definitely the place to see and be seen.

Cyprus Handicraft Centre
At the eastern end of Athalassa Avenue this state-run centre has artisans at work with their products on sale (*tel: 22 305 024*). (Note that this is too far to walk from the city centre – drive or take a taxi.)

The Mall of Cyprus
This is one of the newest additions to Lefkosia's shopping experiences. Familiar names like Debenhams and IKEA sit alongside fashion stores, shoe shops and furnishing centres. It is just off the junction at Strovolos, where the highway heads due southeast towards Larnaka.

Larnaka
Zinonos Kitieos Street
This is the main shopping district of Larnaka. There is a mixture of shops selling the standard tourist goods as well as stylish boutiques catering for fashion-conscious locals. These include a Marks & Spencer in familiar colours.

The seafront
There are myriad souvenir shops and a couple of small minimarkets, but mainly the seafront is occupied by cafés and pubs.

Lemesos
The hotels stretch for many miles east of Lemesos, and where there are hotels in Cyprus, there are always tourist shops and supermarkets. All the necessary day-to-day items can be bought here, as well as the standard souvenirs.

In the town itself, Agiou Andreou Street is the city's very stylish 'high street'. At its far western end, built into several arches near the castle, is a small

Local pottery makes an interesting gift

Lefkara lace is highly prized

shopping arcade containing chic boutiques and jewellery stores. On **Agiou Andreou** itself, there is a large number of funky boutiques, design shops, interior décor stores and a couple of cutting-edge bookshop-cum-coffee shops. The **Agora** shopping arcade has outlets selling expensive jewellery and handicrafts.

For a wider choice of goods head to **My Mall**, a shiny new shopping mall selling everything from the funkiest fashions to organic cosmetics and the latest techno gadgets. There's a good selection of cafés here, and, if you fancy a break from shopping, why not try its central ice-skating rink? My Mall is well signposted on the port side of town.

On the seafront, a number of shops sell copper goods, lace, pottery and souvenirs.

Pafos
Lower town
This is where the tourist shops are gathered in abundance. Where Leoforos Apostolou Pavlou joins the seafront are several souvenir shops. Then turning left along the shoreline, away from the harbour, is a series of shops selling souvenirs. The more discerning should move on to an area of shops arranged around a courtyard, set back from the road, where there are several sculpture workshops offering something a little bit different, along with quality jewellery and leather.

Upper town
The upper town is a warren of busy streets, with only shops in the pedestrianised area focusing on the tourist. There is a good bookshop off to the right from Nikodimou Mylona Street, but otherwise the shops are standard establishments, selling clothes and shoes.

Other places
Lefkara is the home of lacemaking, but visitors should be careful to ensure that they get the genuine article and not imitations. Lefkara lace is, however, sold all across the island.

Phini, **Kornos** and **Geroskipou** have good pottery shops, especially for larger jars and flowerpots.

Basketware originates from **Liopetri** on the way to Agia Napa, but is again widely available elsewhere.

Food stores
There are food stores everywhere in Cyprus. Visitors will have no trouble buying as they do at home.

The range and standard of fruit in the supermarkets is excellent, although the best places for fruit and vegetables are the markets or roadside fruit sellers. The quality of the latter is usually very high, the seller having usually grown it himself – and quite likely to throw in an extra plum or two if he likes the look of you. The roads up to the mountains are the best sources of such stalls.

NORTHERN CYPRUS

Northern Cyprus may offer a smaller range of goods than the south, but the usual global franchises are starting to open boutiques here, especially in Girne and Lefkoşa. Don't be surprised to see Adidas alongside Billabong. Handicrafts such as basketware and pottery are also good buys.

Despite the island's partition, Lefkara lace from the south can also be purchased.

Turkish-Cypriot Lefkoşa

The main shopping areas are **Girne Caddesi**, **Arasta** pedestrianised area, and the **Galleria Arcade**.

On Girne Caddesi are shops, banks and jewellers. Galleria, which comprises two storeys, has an abundance of sportswear shops.

The Arasta pedestrian area is the liveliest and most interesting place to explore. There are lots of textile shops, including some where you can get a suit made. There are also carpenters and leather merchants all around the city. Otherwise, the main things to look for are clothes, jewellery, pottery and crafts.

Gazimağusa

The streets leading to Lala Mustafa Paşa Mosque have some atmospheric old shops selling hand-knitted mohair sweaters, high-quality leather coats and bags, ceramics and brassware. However, as this is a vibrant university town you can expect lots of hip boutiques selling street wear, CDs and mobile phones.

Girne

Hürriyet Caddesi has several stores selling carpets, oriental lamps, pottery, ceramics, brass and copper products. Women will also find leatherware and jewellery worth buying. However, the most popular souvenir among tourists is the mobile phone, cheaper here than in the UK.

The busy shopping centre of Girne Caddesi in Turkish-occupied Lefkoşa (Nicosia)

Entertainment

Cyprus is one of the liveliest holiday islands in the Mediterranean, with lots of nightlife to suit all budgets (and tastes) throughout the summer – though winters are quieter. Most of the island's large hotels host regular 'folkloric' events with troupes of professionals performing traditional Cypriot music and dance. The Middle Eastern influence is strong in Lemesos, and in the Turkish-Cypriot north where Lebanese and Egyptian belly dancers often perform in restaurants and bars.

Lefkosia is not a resort town and special entertainment for visitors is rare. The Municipal Theatre stages plays in Greek and English, and also concerts, and the British Council puts on various entertainments by visiting theatre companies and celebrities. There are, of course, nightclubs and bars in abundance.

Larnaka, and especially Pafos and Lemesos, have a buoyant cultural scene, with numerous art galleries and music venues welcoming tourists as well as locals. There are regular fashion events and musical shows.

Restaurants and bars provide plenty of entertainment too. Pafos's liveliest street is Agiou Antoniou, affectionately known as Bar Street, where there are late-night clubs and music bars. Lemesos's nightlife strip is Leoforos Georgiou I, where the action is in multilevel, multi-ethnic music and sports pubs rather than in dance clubs.

There's also a seedier side. Cyprus has its share of 'hostess clubs'; these have boomed since the collapse of the Soviet Union, which brought an influx of new Russian money. Agia Napa earned a reputation for out-of-control dance clubs and youth mayhem in the late 1990s and early 2000s. The scene has calmed down since local authorities clamped down on late-night clubbing, drug use and public drunkenness, but Agia Napa is still the island's top spot for youngsters.

In north Cyprus, Girne has a preponderance of casinos. Many simply house a collection of one-armed bandits and pin tables; however, a number have roulette and blackjack. As in the south, there is a choice of nightclubs and bars.

The *Monthly Events* guide from the Cyprus Tourism Organisation (CTO) is available at hotels and tourist offices. Also of use are the CTO's annual Diary of Events, listing holidays and organised activities, and their *Traveller's Handbook*. These can be obtained from any CTO office in Cyprus and abroad.

CINEMAS

The Cyprus cinema-going scene has been revived with the opening of multiplex cinema complexes showing the latest English-language releases with Greek subtitles. Call the central ticket office on 77 778 383 for schedules and reservations at any of the K-Cineplex cinemas in Lemesos, Larnaka and Lefkosia.

Larnaka
K-Cineplex
Peloponissou 1 and Indou Potamou.
Tel: 77 778 383.

Lefkosia
Cine Studio Intercollege
Makedonitissis 46.
Tel: 22 358 662.
K-Cineplex 1–6
Makedonitissis 115.
Tel: 77 778 383.
K-Cineplex – The Mall of Cyprus
Verginas 3.
Tel: 77 778 383.
Opera 1, 2
Chr. Sozou 9.
Tel: 22 665 305.
Pantheon Art Cinema
Diagorou 29.
Tel: 22 675 787.

Zena Palace
Th. Theodotou 18.
Tel: 22 674 128.

Lemesos
K-Cineplex 1–5
Ariadnis 8, Mouttagiaka.
Tel: 77 778 383.
Othello 1, 2
Thessalonikis 19.
Tel: 25 352 232.
RIO 1, 2, 3
Ellados 125.
Tel: 25 871 410.

Pafos
Cine Orasis 1, 2
Apostolou Pavlou.
Tel: 26 951 325.
Othellos Cinema
Evagora Pallikaridi 41.
Tel: 26 946 256.

Paralimni
Odeon Cinema
Tel: 23 820 800.

CLUBS AND BARS
Agia Napa
Carwash
This club has a decidedly retro feel but has survived where other dance venues have fallen by the wayside. Nostalgic dance music from the golden 1980s, mixed with more recent sounds.

Agias Mavris 24.
Tel: 23 723 029.
www.carwashcyprus.com
Castle Club
For more than 20 years this large club, complete with 14 bars, a chill-out zone and its own DJ academy, has been an integral part of the local scene. Sounds include Hip Hop, R&B and House.
Louka Louka 20–22.
Tel: 96 386 018.
www.thecastleclub.com
Grease
Disco tops the bill at this outlandish but hugely fun venue not far from Nissi Beach. It gets going from 1pm onwards.
Nissi Beach.
Tel: 23 724 240.
P'zazz
The daddy of Agia Napa's clubs, P'zazz is a legend. It imports top DJs and hosts the biggest and best club events from June to September.
Kryou Nerou 10.
Tel: 23 722 266.

Larnaka
Club Deep
If you love salsa, then this is the club for you. Take a lesson and then

stay on for an evening of dancing every Wednesday.
Leoforos Thinon.
Tel: 99 301 743.

Lefkosia
Agora club

House and R&B are specialities at this stylish nightspot, which is usually full of trendy city types.
Stasinou 11.
Tel: 22 660 179.

Enallax

Greek music features on Thursdays while genres from reggae to classic pop get dancers moving on Fridays. Special theme music nights throughout the week.
Athinas 16.
Tel: 22 430 121.

Ithaki Venue

Housed in a period building in the capital's old town, this is a late-night music club where you can dance to disco and rock. An outdoor bar is open in summer.
Nikiforou Foka 33.
Tel: 22 434 193.
www.ithakivenue.com

Lemesos
The Half Note

Away from the tourist traps on Georgiou I, the Half Note serves up Latin sounds to a dedicated local crowd at weekends, with live bands from time to time.
Socratous 4.
Tel: 25 377 050.

Hippodrome

Living up to its London namesake (or at least trying to), the Hippodrome imports its hits and DJs from the UK and attracts a friendly, fun-seeking summer clientele.
Georgiou 73.
Tel: 25 326 464.

Privilege

As far as locals are concerned, this huge venue is the epicentre of Lemesos nightlife, with several dance areas and DJs spinning a mix of Euro-imports and Greek anthems.
Lefkosia–Lemesos motorway, 3km (2 miles) east of Amathous.
Tel: 25 634 040.

Step Inn

The biggest Irish pub in Cyprus sprawls over four floors offering satellite TV screens that show everything from ten-pin bowling to tractor pulls. It also has snooker and pool tables, darts, karaoke and, of course, ice-cold Guinness®.
Georgiou 89.
Tel: 25 325 389.
www.stepinnbar.com

Zygos Gentlemen's Club

If live shows featuring scantily clad girls is your thing, then this venue will be sure to please.
Leoforos Makarios.
Tel: 25 579 851.

Catch a colourful parade at Lemesos Carnival

Pafos

You can get (pretty much) anything you want in the way of nightlife on Agiou Antoniou, from R&B to 1970s diva disco sounds. Just don't bother turning up before midnight.

Gallery

Gallery is laid-back and youthful, and its DJs place their emphasis on garage and R&B. It has been on the scene here almost as long as the rival Rainbow.

Agiou Antoniou.

Rainbow

The street's longest-established and hardest-to-miss club – just look for the big rainbow sign. Latest dance sounds and DJs from Britain, Belgium, Germany and Holland.

Agiou Antoniou.

Red Cube

Separating the committed clubber from the mere amateur, Red Cube doesn't even open until midnight. Don't go unless you are up for a good five hours of R&B, soul, garage and more.

Tombs of the Kings Road.

CULTURAL CENTRES AND THEATRES

Agia Napa

Plateia Seferi

Performances of music and dance are held here throughout the summer, mainly on Sundays. The Agia Napa Festival is its highlight.

Larnaka

Larnaka Municipal Theatre

This theatre is at the heart of the town's cultural scene, and hosts performances as diverse as plays for children to orchestral, choir and theatrical events.

Leoforos Grigori Afxentiou. Tel: 24 665 794.

Lefkosia

To Skali Amphitheatre

The setting for a programme of folkloric and modern performances, especially in summer.

Aglantzia. Tel: 22 336 363.

Strovolos Municipal Theatre

Performances range from operatic to ballet at this popular venue.

Leoforos Strovolou 100. Tel: 22 313 010.

Lemesos

Ancient Kourion Amphitheatre

A programme of magical theatre performances is held here in the summer. Details appear in the local press and are held by hotel concierges and tourist offices.

Rialto Theatre

This super theatre hosts dance performances and competitions, musical events and festivals, ballet and cinema.

Andrea Drousioti 19, Heroes Square. Tel: 77 777 745. www.railto.com.cy

Pafos

Pafos harbour

Regular cultural events, including the annual opera held in front of the castle. Information available from the local press and the tourist offices.

Markeidion Theatre

Performances by classical and orchestral musicians, along with special musical theatre events, make this a popular venue.

Andrea Geroudi 27. Tel: 26 932 571.

Food and drink

Owning a restaurant seems to be the main occupation of an enormous number of Cypriots: from small ramshackle tavernas to sophisticated cosmopolitan establishments, there is a multitude of places to eat. Service is usually attentive and efficient, and there is a wide range of dishes available, both traditional Cypriot, Greek, Turkish and international. The Cypriots make brave attempts at providing translations, but these can have entertaining results.

FOOD

To really experience traditional Cypriot food at its best, head for a taverna, ideally in one of the island's villages where recipes have been handed down through the generations. If dishes like *afelia*, *kleftiko* or *sheftalia* (slow-cooked pork in red wine with coriander, lamb with herbs, and sausages respectively) leave you a little perplexed as to what to try, why not opt for a *mezedhes* (known as a meze).

Waiters will bring a steady stream of small dishes of food to your table, sometimes as many as 25. The meze will start with dips, bread and a village salad, followed by local meat, fish and vegetable dishes. To finish, you will probably be served a local cake or fruit. It's a great way to try lots of different Cypriot dishes in one go, and if there's something you don't like, there are plenty of alternatives.

A very similar range of food is available on the Turkish side of the island. Turkish cuisine is more complex, spicy and rich, because of their contact with the Persians and Arabs. There are delicious snack mezes and some good fresh fish dishes. Kebab is lamb roasted on a skewer and served with rice. Doner-kebab is lamb or beef roasted on a turning skewer and then cut in thin slices.

Soups

Avgolemono: chicken stock with rice, egg and lemon.
Psarosoupa: fish and vegetable soup.

Meze and dips

Dolmades: stuffed vine leaves.
Hummus: chickpea dip.
Tahini: sesame-seed paste.
Taramasalata: smoked cod's roe.
Tzatziki: yoghurt, cucumber and mint dip.

Meat dishes

Afelia: pork marinated in red wine.
Beef stifado: beef casserole in red wine.
Kleftiko: slow-roasted lamb cooked in a traditional *kleftiko* oven.

Kotopoulo: chicken.

Lamb tavas: lamb casserole.

Lounza: smoked pork (like bacon) served grilled.

Pork souvlaki (kebab): meat on skewers served with salad and pitta bread.

Souvlakia: large pieces of lamb or pork spit-roasted over charcoal.

Other meat dishes

Full kebab: a northern Cypriot feast of kebabs, sausages and grilled meats.

Keftedes: meatballs.

Kypriakes ravioles: ravioli stuffed with halloumi cheese.

Moussaka: minced lamb with layers of potatoes and aubergines in béchamel sauce.

Sheftalia: a type of sausage often served with souvlakia, in pitta bread.

Fish and seafood

Being so close to the sea, fish is always fresh. In good fish restaurants you can select the particular fish you want. Octopus usually comes steamed in red wine.

Barbounia: red mullet.

Kalimari: squid in rings.

Xyphias: swordfish.

Salads

Salads accompany most meals. The ingredients tend to depend on season but usually contain tomatoes, cucumber and feta cheese. What is known as Greek salad in Greece tends to be known as village salad in southern Cyprus.

The northern Cypriots love their Shepherd's Salad, or *choban*, which often includes grated carrot.

The ubiquitous outdoor café

Cheese

Feta: white cheese made from sheep's milk, usually found in Greek salad.
Halloumi: squeaky white cheese made from goat's milk. This is popular fried.

Sweets

Baklava: filo pastry with cinnamon, nuts and syrup.
Kadaiffi: a similar sweet with a shredded wheat-like casing.
Lokoumi: Turkish Delight.

Fruit

There is always a tempting selection of fruit available in Cyprus; seasonal fruit is often served as a dessert.

Coffee

Coffee is drunk throughout the day and served at the end of most meals, on request. There is a wide range of types from Nescafé to Greek coffee and Turkish coffee, served in small cups in three strengths; medium, sweet or unsweetened.

Cake shops

Expect a huge range of sweet cakes and biscuits wrapped to take away or simply to be eaten on the spot, accompanied by a glass of water. Many bakeries stay open 24 hours.

DRINK

A fine selection of increasingly popular wines is available on the island. The only appellation-controlled wine is Commandaria St John. It is a fortified dessert wine, first produced in the Middle Ages for the Knights of St John at Kolossi. Much was exported, and it was apparently appreciated by the Plantagenet kings of England.

Most of the island's wines are dry to medium dry, and there is a huge selection to choose from.

There is also a good range of wines available in the north, although the wine industry is in its infancy. Kantára white and red are the most widely available.

Light beers are a very popular way of quenching thirst on a hot day. The locally made Keo and Carlsberg are on offer everywhere in the south. Imported beers and lagers are also readily obtainable but are more expensive.

Ouzo and raki are the most popular local drinks. The aniseed flavour perfectly accompanies Cypriot cuisine.

WHERE TO EAT

Restaurants in Cyprus reflect the island's cosmopolitan clientele, and genuine Cypriot tavernas are outnumbered by Italian pizzerias, French-influenced 'international' restaurants, British-style pubs and fish and chip shops, Indian, Thai, Japanese and Chinese restaurants, and a growing number of restaurants catering to the tastes of Russian, Polish and other eastern European visitors. Proximity to Lebanon also ensures a substantial number of Middle Eastern-flavoured places.

There are several vegetarian places on Cyprus; however, vegetarians will find a wide choice of salads, fruit and various dips in restaurant menus, and most meze restaurants, which serve a variety of vegetarian dishes such as hummus and tzatziki, as well as salads.

Even the most expensive eating places are affordable by most European standards, and the more modest establishments are within even the tightest holiday budget. Often, the most expensive places to eat are those serving high-quality local dishes to a discerning Cypriot clientele, while Italian-style pizzerias and other 'international' restaurants catering to a purely tourist audience are much cheaper.

In the main tourist hubs – Agia Napa, Pafos, Protaras, Lemesos and Larnaka – Chinese and Indian restaurants and pizzerias offer takeaway and free home delivery meals for those in self-catering accommodation.

Locally made beers, wines and spirits are cheaper than imported drinks. Imported wines are often cheaper than Cypriot wines. The local beers and spirits are perfectly drinkable too.

Restaurant prices in Turkish Cyprus are more expensive than the south.

In the south, the currency is the euro, while in the north restaurant prices in tourist areas are usually given in euros, dollars and sterling, all of which are accepted as well as the Turkish lira.

Meze are typical of Greek cuisine

In the following list of recommended restaurants, the price rating indicates the approximate cost per person for a meal.

£ Up to €20/YTL38
££ €20–60/YTL38–115
£££ Over €60/YTL115

LEFKOSIA

Zanettos £
This secret gem is a local institution, offering an extravagant feast of meze and meat dishes.
Trikoupi 65.
Tel: 22 765 501.

Abu Faysal ££
A taste of Lebanon in the heart of Lefkosia.
Klementos 31.
Tel: 22 763 650.

Aegean ££
Highly regarded for Greek-Cypriot dishes, especially the meze.
Ektoros 40.
Tel: 22 433 297.

Bagatelle ££
Complete with pianist, serves refined French cuisine.
Kyrakos Matsis 16.
Tel: 22 317 870.

Bistrot 1900 ££
An elegant French bistro serving up fine steaks and Mediterranean cuisine to a jazz soundtrack.
Plateia Eleftherias.
Tel: 22 667 668.

Brasserie Au Bon Plaisir £££
Delicious French dishes and fine wines.
Alasias 15.
Tel: 22 755 111.

Marco Polo £££
This rooftop restaurant is famous for its extensive sushi and fish buffet.
Regaena 70.
Tel: 22 712 712.

SOUTHEAST

Agia Napa

Fotiana Restaurant £
Traditional Cypriot dishes like souvlakia have made this restaurant highly popular.
Tefkrou Athia 32.
Tel: 23 721 135.

Le Bistro d'Hier ££
With an eclectic French menu featuring vegetarian dishes, this bistro is one of the best in Agia Napa.
Odyseos Elitis 11.
Tel: 23 721 838.

La Casa di Napa ££
Italian food at its best.
Solomou 8.
Tel: 23 722 137.

Limelight Taverna ££
Seafood and red meat from the charcoal grill.
Lipetris 11.
Tel: 23 721 650.

Pagoda ££
Renowned for its superb Chinese food. Booking essential in peak season.
Leoforos Nissi 29.
Tel: 23 819 988.

Vassos £££
Beside Agia Napa harbour, Vassos is the best of a clutch of seafood restaurants and is well established.
Leoforos Archiepiskopou Makariou III.
Tel: 23 721 884.

Larnaka

Ammos £
Tuck into a fresh light salad then swing yourself to sleep on a hammock.
Mackenzie Beach.
Tel: 24 828 844.

Art Café 1900 £
A good vegetarian menu and fresh juices as well as traditional choices.
Stasinou 6.
Tel: 24 653 027.

Habibi £
This buzzy Lebanese restaurant serves up

excellent-value Arabic meze. Belly dancing shows at weekends.
Avgerinou 10.
Tel: 70 003 222.

Metz Café Bar £
This café-bar is great for light meals and snacks on the move.
Lordou Vironos 5–6.
Tel: 24 823 770.

Militzis £
One of the best traditional tavernas in town, and a great place to sample local food.
Piyale Paşa 42.
Tel: 24 655 867.

Moti Mahal £
Tasty Indian-fusion cuisine served up in atmospheric Rajasthani décor.
Leoforos Athinon 52.
Tel: 70 004 484.

Black Turtle ££
The place to go for an 'authentic' Cypriot night out, with live music, dancing and occasional plate-smashing.
11 Mehmet Ali.
Tel: 24 650 661.

Paradosiako ££
Good seafood and meze at this very affordable waterfront restaurant.
Sakaria 2.
Tel: 24 658 318.

Salamis Restaurant ££
Right by Mackenzie Beach, this elegant taverna has a wide choice of fresh fish dishes and steaks. A fine wine list, excellent ales and a cocktail bar complete the package.
Mackenzie Beach.
Tel: 24 623 761.

Varoshiotis Seafood ££
This family-owned chain is beloved by the locals – expect enormous portions of freshly caught seafood.
Piyale Paşa 7.
Tel: 77 777 708.

Krateon £££
For a special treat, this French restaurant is hard to beat. Reservations are strongly recommended.
Kimonos 21.
Tel: 24 622 062.

Larnaka–Dekelia Road

Les Etoiles ££
Formal restaurant which attracts those looking for stylish atmosphere.
Opposite Golden Bay Hotel. Tel: 24 646 777.

Protaras and Paralimni

Platea £
More a café than a restaurant, but with a very good menu of Cypriot snacks and light meals.
Leoforos Archiepiskopou Makariou III 10.
Tel: 23 740 190.

Il Cavaliere ££
Family-friendly restaurant with a good range of Italian dishes.
Pernera 6.
Tel: 23 831 022.

La Cultura del Gusto ££
Lively and colourfully decorated, this restaurant near the sea specialises in Italian regional dishes.
Ifestou 7.
Tel: 23 833 860.

São Paulo ££
The only Brazilian restaurant in the area, with a flamboyant supper show.
Xenodohion 43.
Tel: 23 832 610.

SOUTH

Lemesos

Alianda £
The best-value dinner in Lemesos, with outdoor garden dining in summer and pleasant indoor dining rooms as well.

Food and drink

Irinis 117.
Tel: 25 340 758.

Kapillio Tavern £
This village taverna
serves a great meze,
along with traditional
dishes like *kleftiko.*
Agios Tychonas village
centre.
Tel: 25 315 115.

Caprice ££
The light Mediterranean-
Italian cuisine is well
matched with the bright,
chic interior. Try the
Cypriot wines.
Londa Hotel, Georgiou I 72.
Tel: 25 865 555. Open:
daily dinner only.

Molly Malone's Irish
Pub and Restaurant ££
Big-screen televisions
showing live sports
events, light meals and,
of course, Irish beers
combine to make this a
lively place to relax.
Located on the outskirts
of Lemesos.
Amathoundos 180,
Parekklisia.
Tel: 25 821 082.

Ta Piatakia ££
Popular restaurant with
a contemporary take on
traditional meze. Book
ahead for a table.
Nikodimou Mylona 5.
Tel: 25 745 017.

Porta Tavern ££
Housed in a period
building in the centre of
the old town, this taverna
is known for its summer
barbecue events.
Genethliou Mitella 17.
Tel: 25 360 339.

La Maison Fleurie £££
This elegant restaurant is
ideal for a special meal.
Its menu is varied and
features French dishes
and wines.
Christaki Kranou 18.
Tel: 25 320 680.

Mavromatis £££
Outstanding Greek
cuisine in an elegant
restaurant. The service is
exemplary and the wine
list superb.
Four Seasons Hotel,
Leoforos Amathous.
Tel: 25 858 000. Open:
Mon–Sat dinner only.

Terra e Mare £££
Another buffet place that's
popular with expats.
Amathounto 198.
Tel: 25 635 343.

Vivaldi £££
Possibly Cyprus's finest
dining experience. Expect
classic Italian with a twist.
Four Seasons Hotel,
Leoforos Amathous.
Tel: 25 858 000. Open:
Tue–Sun dinner only.

Zen Room £££
A calm ambience and
oriental décor provide
the perfect canvas for
serving delicious Thai
and Japanese dishes.
Leoforos Amathous.
Tel: 25 812 659.

WEST
Pafos
Gina's £
Excellent coffee, salads,
snacks and desserts.
Agios Antonios 3.
Tel: 26 938 017.

Café Vienna ££
Coffee and cakes in
pleasant surroundings.
Leoforos Poseidonos 12.
Tel: 26 943 313.

Cavallini ££
Fine Italian cuisine and
excellent service.
Leoforos Poseidonos 65.
Tel: 26 964 164.

Colosseum Ristorante
Italiano ££
Creatively presented
Italian dishes are
complemented by fine
wines at this stylish
steakhouse with regular
entertainment.
Danaes 20.
Tel: 26 913 278.

Demokritos ££
The oldest restaurant in
Pafos, Demokritos is

known for its welcoming feel, delicious menu of local dishes and its nightly performances of traditional Cypriot music and dance.
Dionysou 1.
Tel: 26 933 371.

Jade Palace ££
A spacious and elegant restaurant, the Jade Palace in Pegeia village has a wide menu of classic Chinese dishes. Its set menus offer great value.
Laxion 24, Pegeia.
Tel: 26 621 829.

Mandra Tavern ££
Locals and tourists alike love this traditional taverna for its hearty, rustic Greek and Cypriot dishes.
4 Dionysou, Kato Pafos.
Tel: 26 934 129.

Petradaki ££
Hosts Bambos and Niki offer an elegant restaurant with views over vineyards, and a menu of classic Cypriot dishes with a modern twist.
Kato Vrisi 45, Kathikas.
Tel: 26 814 191.

Phuket ££
Chinese-Thai cuisine.
44 Tafon ton Vasileon.
Tel: 26 936 738.

Seagull ££
Located right by the sea, this Kato Pafos restaurant is bright and welcoming.
Leoforos Poseidonos 7.
Tel: 26 950 489.

St George Fish Tavern ££
This old-fashioned tavern by the harbour at Agios Georgios has the freshest fish in the area.
Agios Georgios, Pegeia.
Tel: 26 621 888.

Yiannis Taverna ££
Sample local dishes and enjoy a welcome from Yiannis himself in this atmospheric stone-built taverna in the wine village of Kathikas.
Georgiou Kleanthous 11, Kathikas.
Tel: 26 633 353.

Pavarotti £££
One of the more expensive choices in Pafos, but the excellent Italian food is worth it.
Othellou 5.
Tel: 26 912 588.

Polis area
Yiangos & Peter Taverna £
Freshly caught seafood and tasty meze.
Latchi harbour, Latchi.
Tel: 26 321 411.

Old Town £££
Expensive and stylish, a cut above the majority of local restaurants.
Kyprolondeos 9.
Tel: 26 322 758.

TROODOS
Kakopetria
Mill Hotel Restaurant ££
Varied cuisine; succulent, local trout.
Tel: 22 922 536.

Platres
Kaledonia ££
Traditional dishes.
31 Olympou, Pano Platres. Tel: 25 421 404.

NORTH
Girne area
The Abbey Bell Tower ££
Enjoy classic Turkish-Cypriot and Mediterranean dishes in this first-floor restaurant looking out over Bellapaïs Abbey.
Bellapaïs village centre, near Girne (Kyrenia).
Tel: 815 7507.

Canlı Balık ££
Specialises in fresh fish dishes served with a few well-chosen herbs.
Girne (Kyrenia) harbour.
Tel: 815 2182.

Children

There are a great many parks and places of interest for children to enjoy all over the island, as well as the virtues of sea, sand and warm weather. The Cypriots love children and they are welcome everywhere.

Agia Napa
WaterWorld
One of Europe's largest water parks with rides and attractions to suit all ages.
Off the Agia Thekla road, 5km (3 miles) west of Agia Napa. Tel: 23 724 444. www.waterworldwaterpark.com. Open: Mar–mid-Nov daily 10am–6pm.
Yellow Submarine
Not quite the real thing, but the underwater views from the submarine's lower deck are terrific.
Agia Napa harbour. Tel: 99 658 280. Departures: 10.30am, noon & 2.30pm, but times can vary.

Larnaka
Camel Park
Set in landscaped gardens, this park offers the chance for children to learn more about camels. They can even feed them and enjoy a camel ride. See ponies, deer, kangaroos and ostriches too. Refreshments, a swimming pool and play areas are on-site.
Mazotos, near Larnaka. Tel: 24 991 243.

www.camel-park.com. Open: summer daily 9am–7pm; winter daily 9am–5pm.
Karting Centre
Mini-track of 220m (240yds) with a main track of 1.6km (1 mile).
Dromolaxia, 6km (4 miles) southwest of Larnaka. Tel: 70 007 677. Open: daily 9am–midnight.

Lemesos
Cyprus Donkey Sanctuary
Home to more than 120 rescued donkeys and mules.
Vouni village on the outskirts of Lemesos. Tel: 25 945 488. www.donkeysanctuarycyprus.org. Open: daily 10am–4pm.
Fasouri Water Mania
Slides, chutes and pools, plus picnic areas and restaurants, can be found at this large water park.
Off the road from Lemesos new port to Pafos, through the village of Trahoni. Tel: 25 714 235. www.fasouri-watermania.com. Open: May–Oct daily 10am–6pm.

Lemesos Zoo
The only zoo in Cyprus.
Municipal Gardens, Oktovriou 28, Lemesos. Open: daily 9am–6.30pm.

The Need 4 Speed
A go-karting track with sessions designed to suit different age groups.
Erimi village centre, outskirts of Lemesos. Tel: 99 462 269. Open: daily 9am–midnight.

Reptile House
Native lizards and other exotic specimens are on display.
Old harbour, Lemesos. Open: daily 9am–6.30pm.

Wild Valley Resort Ostrich Farm
Ostriches, deer and other animals provide plenty of entertainment.
On the Pissouri–Plataniskia road, outskirts of Lemesos. Tel: 25 991 010. Open: daily 9am–sunset.

Pafos

Aphrodite Waterpark
Water slides and chutes.
Off Leoforos Poseidonos, Geroskipou, Kato Palos. Tel: 26 913 638. www. aphroditewaterpark.com. Open: May– Jun daily 10am–5.30pm; Jul–Aug daily 10am–6pm; Sept–Oct daily 10am–5pm.

CitySightseeing Pafos
Families will love the chance to see the sights from an open-top bus.
Pafos harbour. Tel: 99 393 766. www.cypruscitysightseeing.com. Tours depart daily 10am–4pm.

Pafos Bird and Animal Park
Many varieties of exotic birds and animals.
On the road between Ormos Korallion (Coral Bay) and Agios Georgiou, Pegeia, near Pafos. Tel: 26 813 852. Open: Apr–Sept daily 9am–8pm; Oct–Mar daily 9am–5pm.

Pafos Karting Centre
A fun track where all the family can have a go.
Off Leoforos Poseidonos near the Riu Cypria Maris Hotel. Tel: 70 000 807.

Roskos Karting Centre
This track is easy to find, near the Aphrodite Waterpark.
Off Leoforos Poseidonos. Tel: 99 613 050.

Snake George Reptile Park
Snake George has a collection of over 100 snakes and other reptiles, many native to Cyprus. At the time of writing he is relocating to new premises in Pafos so he can create a conservation exhibition and information area. Call Snake George to check up-to-date information.
Tel: 99 987 685. www.snakegeorge.com

Paralimni

Ocean Aquarium Protaras
Over 400 species of marine life are kept in this family-friendly attraction.
Leoforos Kavo Gkreko, Protaras, 5km (3 miles) north of the resort centre. Tel: 23 741 111. Open: daily 10am–6pm.

Protaras Fun Park
Water attractions designed for children under 14 years.
On the seafront next to the Paschalia Hotel. Tel: 23 833 888. Open: Apr–Oct daily 10am–6pm.

Sport and leisure

Cyprus offers a wide variety of activities to get stuck into if you like your holidays on the active side. The most obvious option is hiking around the Troodos Mountains, Akamas Peninsula or other wild areas, but centres for other participation and spectator sports are scattered around the island, offering everything from diving to skiing.

ANGLING

Fishing is permitted in numerous reservoirs around the island and licences can be obtained from the district offices of the Fisheries Department listed below. Species are trout, carp, mosquito fish, perch, catfish and silver bream.

Larnaka and the southeast
Leoforos Piale Pasha, Larnaka. Tel: 24 823 407, 24 304 294.

Lefkosia and the High Troodos
Vithleem 101, Lefkosia. Tel: 22 807 830.

Lemesos and the south
Lemesos harbour. Tel: 25 817 312.

Pafos and the west
Pafos harbour. Tel: 26 815 849, 26 306 268.

Sea fishing is also possible from the main coastal resorts, and amateur anglers do not need a licence, although there are restrictions on the number of hooks permitted and the species that you may catch.

ARCHERY
Lemesos and the south
Santa Marina Retreat
Near Parekklisia, Lemesos. Tel: 99 535 000.

ATHLETICS
Although Cyprus is not at the forefront of world athletics, track and field events are popular and many Cypriots take a regular run or jog.

Larnaka
GSZ Stadium
Eight-lane, 400m (¼-mile) tartan track.
3km (2 miles) west of town centre. Tel: 24 532 602.

Lefkosia
GSP Stadium
Modern stadium completed in 2003.
Strovolos, junction 6 of the Lefkosia–Lemesos motorway. Tel: 22 515 044.

Makarios Athletic Centre

Makedonitissa, 6km (4 miles) southeast of city centre. Tel: 22 897 000.

Lemesos (Limassol)
Tsirion Stadium

Eight-lane, 400m (¼-mile) tartan track, 40m (130ft) indoor track.
Kavounidou, 5km (3 miles) northwest of the town centre. Tel: 25 387 370.

Pafos
Pafiako Athletic Centre

Leoforos Makariou 91, Geroskipou. Tel: 22 897 000.

BADMINTON
Contact **Cyprus Badminton Federation** (*tel: 22 449 868; www.cyprusbadminton.com*).

BASKETBALL
Contact **Cyprus Basketball Federation** (*tel: 22 449 830; www.basketball.org.cy*).

BOATING
There's a good choice of fun to be had on the water. Among the options are glass-bottom boats, cruisers and catamarans. Pedalos are hugely popular, especially with children.

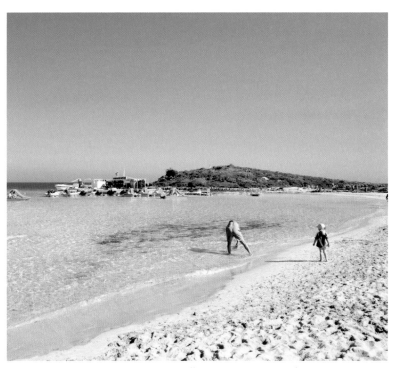

Beaches and seaside resorts such as Protaras offer limitless opportunities for watersports

Sport and leisure

Agia Napa

Glass-bottom boats offer hour-long trips that allow you to discover the underwater world. More conventional craft offer half- and one-day excursions around Cape Gkreko and north into Gazimağusa Bay. Enquire at **Agia Napa harbour** (*open: Apr–Oct daily*).

Lemesos and the south

Catamaran Cruises from Lemesos Old Port to Cape Gata. **Relax Catamaran Cruises** (*tel: 99 562 074*).

Pafos and the west

Glass-bottom boats go out to small rocky islands and wrecks off Pafos. Trips last about an hour. More conventional crafts take passengers up the west coast to Agios Georgios and further. Enquire at **Pafos harbour** (*open: Apr–Oct daily*) and also **Paphos Sea Cruises** (*tel: 26 910 200*).

BOWLING (TEN PIN)

Cyprus Bowling Association
General information.
PO Box 50642, Lemesos. www.cbf.com.cy

Larnaka and the southeast

Rock'n'Bowl
Fifteen lanes, billiards and music.
Dekeleia Rd, opposite Beau Rivage Hotel, Larnaka. Tel: 24 822 777. Open: daily 10am–midnight.

Virtuality Bowling Center
Eleftherias 24, Agia Napa. Tel: 23 723 290. Open: daily 10am–midnight.

Lemesos and the south

Space Bowling
Sixteen lanes, a TV screen and all the latest technology plus a restaurant.
Hercules 1, Germasogeia, motorway junction 23 area, Lemesos. Tel: 25 310 000. Open: daily 10am–2am.

Pafos and the west

Cockatoos
Ten lanes, pool, snooker and a cafeteria.
Ayiou Antoniou 25, Kato Pafos. Tel: 26 822 004. Open: daily 10am–3am.

CYCLING

Bikes can be hired in the resorts. The **Cyprus Tourism Organisation** in Lefkosia issues a booklet with various routes described. For further information, you can contact the **Cyprus Cycling Federation** (*tel: 22 449 870*) or the **Lemesos Cycling Club** (*tel: 25 585 980*).

CYPRUS RALLY

The Cyprus Rally is rated the most difficult round of the FIA World Rally Championship and features the world's best rally drivers. Spectator viewing spots are set close to the special stages in the Troodos Mountains. For scheduling information contact **Cyprus Automobile Association** (*tel: 22 313 233; www.caa.com.cy*).

DIVING

There are sub-aqua clubs and diving centres in resorts and some hotels. For further information contact:

The south
Cyprus Federation of Underwater Activities
PO Box 21503, Lefkosia. Tel: 22 754 647.
For Lemesos **Dive-In**
Tel: 25 311 600. www.dive-in.com.cy
For Pafos **Cydive**
Tel: 24 665 408. www.cydive.com

The north
Amphora Scuba Diving Center
Tel: 851 4924.
www.amphoradiving.com

FOOTBALL
Cyprus has an established league structure with pitches in the main towns.

Lefkosia's GSP Stadium is very modern and seats 26,000. It is used for league and international matches.
Junction 6 off the Lefkosia–Lemesos motorway.

Lemesos's Tsirion Stadium hosts major league games.
5km (3 miles) north of town centre, off the Lefkosia–Lemesos motorway.

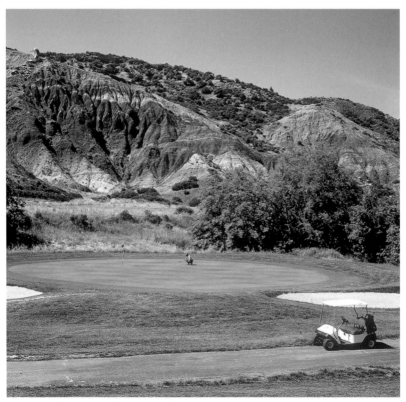

The lush greenery of the Secret Valley Golf Club

GOLF

Cyprus has seen several courses develop over the past few years, and more are planned.

Lemesos
Vikla Golf and Country Club
25km (15½ miles) northeast of Lemesos, Parekklisia exit from motorway, Vikla. Tel: 25 622 894. www.vikla4golf.com

Pafos
Aphrodite Hills
25km (15½ miles) east of Pafos, near Petra tou Romiou. Tel: 26 828 000. www.aphroditehills.com
Secret Valley Golf Club
20km (12½ miles) east of Pafos, near Petra tou Romiou. Tel: 26 642 774.
Tsada Golf Club
Tsada, 12km (7½ miles) northeast of Pafos. Tel: 26 642 774, 26 642 775. www.cyprusgolf.com

The north
Esentepe Golf Course
Korineum Golf and Country Club, Esentepe, near Girne. Tel: 600 1500. www.korineumgolf.com

HANG-GLIDING

Centres for hang-gliding can be found around the island's coast, where you can also enjoy parascending – meaning that, at extravagant cost, the laws of gravity can be suspended for a circuit of the bay. It all seems to work, the only problem being a likely ducking on descent. It's great fun though.

Lemesos and the south
The main site is Kourion sea cliffs. For more information on hang-gliding and airsports, contact **Cyprus Airsports Federation** (*tel: 22 339 771; www.caf.org.cy*).

The north
Highline Paragliding
This team of highly experienced and licensed professional pilots has been offering paragliding in northern Cyprus for nine years, to all ages and levels.
Office on Kyrenia harbour. Tel: 855 5672. www.highlineparagliding.com

HORSE RACING

There is racing throughout the year.
Lefkosia Racecourse
Ippodromion, west of city centre. Tel: 22 782 727. www.nicosiaraceclub.com.cy

HORSE RIDING

Obtain information from **Cyprus Equestrian Federation** (*tel: 22 872 172*).

Larnaka and the southeast
Moonshine Ranch
Kavo Gkreko Rd, opposite Grecian Bay Hotel, Agia Napa. Tel: 99 605 042.

Lefkosia
Nicosia Riding Club
Lythrodontas village, 20km (12½ miles) southwest of Lefkosia. Tel: 99 671 789.

Lemesos and the south
Amathous Park Riding School
Near Parekklisia, junction 21 off the Lefkosia–Lemesos motorway.
Tel: 99 604 109.
Santa Marina Retreat
Near Parekklisia, 10km (6½ miles) northeast of Lemesos. Tel: 99 535 000 ext 317.

Pafos and the west
Ride In Cyprus
Lysos, 32km (20 miles) north of Pafos. Tel: 99 777 624.

The north
Dörtnal Riding Club
Karaoğlanoğlu. Tel: 822 2293.
Riverside HV Horse Riding
Alsancak. Tel: 821 8906.

SAILING
Sailing boats and windsurfers are available on many beaches but are often hard to get hold of.

Larnaka
Larnaka Marina
Tel: 24 653 110.
Larnaka Nautical Club
Dhekelia Rd. Tel: 24 623 399.

Lemesos
St Raphael Marina
Old Lefkosia–Lemesos Rd. Tel: 25 636 100.

Pafos
Pafos Nautical Club
Municipal beach. Tel: 26 233 745.

The north
Girne (Kyrenia) harbour
Berthing for Turkish-Cypriot boats and craft touring the eastern Mediterranean.
Girne Nautical Club
Diana Beach. Tel: 864 1644.

SIGHTSEEING
Look out for excursions to places such as the Troodos Mountains, or you can hire a taxi for a tour of the island. A great way to see the sights and sites of the towns is to take an open-top bus tour.

CitySightseeing Pafos
Part of the worldwide network of bus tours, this excellent 'hop-on hop-off' tour takes in all the major attractions of Pafos.
Pafos harbour. Tel: 99 393 766. www.cypruscitysightseeing.com. Tours depart daily 10am–4pm.

SKIING
Yes, it is possible to ski in Cyprus! But only at Mount Olympos, which, at 1,952m (6,404ft) above sea level, is the only peak that catches the snow. There are four short runs of about 200m (660ft) in length in Sun Valley and on the north face five demanding descents twice the length.

Ski equipment and sledges can be hired in Sub Valley 1. At weekends it is a good idea to get to the slopes early if you need equipment. The season runs from the first week in

January to the end of March although there's no guarantee of snow at any time of year – check the weather report first. The slopes can be reached in about an hour from Lefkosia and Lemesos.

To stay overnight, try Troodos and Platres. For information contact the **Cyprus Ski Club** (*Amfipoleos 21, Lefkosia; tel: 22 449 837; www.cyprusski.com*).

SWIMMING
On every beach, red buoys define the swimming areas. Warning flags (red = danger, yellow = caution, striped red over yellow = safe) indicate the condition of the sea and warnings should be complied with at all times. Three public beaches listed below offer full facilities to swimmers including changing rooms, although of course there are many more beaches. Entrance to beaches is free. There are usually lifeguards between 10am and 6pm.

The sea is warm from June onwards, usually calm and a beautiful turquoise. Those that have mastered the twin arts of breathing through a small tube and keeping their visor clear have a splendid time snorkelling and surveying the wonders of the deep. Most of these beaches have a range of services that include lounger and umbrella hire, beach cafés and restaurants.

Be careful not to overdo the sunbathing, particularly at the beginning of your holiday, during the middle of the day when the sun is strongest, and with children.

Larnaka
Public beach
Pyl, 10km (6 miles) east of Larnaka. Tel: 24 646 244.

Lemesos
Dasoudi public beach
5km (3 miles) east of Lemesos centre. Tel: 25 322 881.

Pafos and the west
Geroskipou
2km (1¼ miles) southeast of Pafos harbour. Tel: 26 964 525.

If visiting Lefkosia, the **Eleon Pool** is open to day members (*3 Ploutarchos St, Ekgomi, 2km/1¼ miles west of city centre; tel: 22 451 445*).

TENNIS
Cyprus Tennis Federation
PO Box 23931, Lefkosia. Tel: 22 449 860. www.cyprustennis.com

The following centres are just a few of many open to the public.

Larnaka
Larnaka Tennis Club
Kilkis 10, town centre. Tel: 24 656 999.

Lefkosia
Eleon
*Ploutarchos 3, Ekgomi, 2km (1¹/4 miles)
west of city centre. Tel: 22 679 923.*
National Tennis Centre
Centre court seats 3,000.
*Leoforos Makarion Stadium.
Tel: 22 356 766.*
Nicosia Tennis Club – Field Club
*Leoforos Aigyptou, city centre.
Tel: 22 668 041.*

Lemesos
Famagusta Tennis Club
Messaorias 3. Tel: 25 335 952.
Herodotou Tennis Academy
Kiliou 8. Tel: 24 654 616.
Sporting Club
Ioannis Zacharidou 4. Tel: 25 564 697.

Pafos
Pafos Tennis Club
Geroskipou Beach. Tel: 99 620 913.

Paralimni
Paralimni Tennis Club
Paralimni. Tel: 99 658 444.

WALKING
The **Cyprus Tourism Organisation**
(*tel: 22 691 100; www.visitcyprus.com*)
produces the excellent 'Cyprus Nature
Trails' brochure with maps, and the even
more impressive 'European Long
Distance Path E4' and other information
on Cyprus Nature Trails.

In northern Cyprus, specialist travel
company **Örnek Holidays** offers
walking tours, birdwatching and
botany treks (*tel: 815 8969;
http://ornekholidays.eu*).

Midsummer is too hot for walking,
with mountain temperatures too
much for most people. Walkers
should take plenty of water with them.
In the winter the mountains can be
cold, wet and cloudy, and Mount
Olympos can be almost arctic, so
proper clothing, footwear and a
compass are required. Large-scale maps
are needed on many walks and the
1:50,000 scale Ministry of Defence
series, K717, is invaluable. Try the
Department of Lands and Surveys
in Lefkosia (*tel: 22 402 890*).

WATERSKIING
Hotels are the best source of boats,
drivers and equipment. Early morning
and late afternoon provide the calmest
water. There can be much waiting
around, but it's worth it.

Protaras often has ideal conditions for
waterskiing, early in the day or late
afternoon. Experienced waterskiers will
be familiar with the situation where the
boat has broken down – they will be told
the boat is coming from the next bay and
the mono-ski will be repaired in a
minute. This is a sport for the patient.

WINDSURFING
All the main beaches have a selection of
boards for hire. Courses of instruction
are a good idea for beginners.
Experienced board sailors will be
disappointed that the strong winds are
infrequent in summer.

Accommodation

Hotels in Cyprus are graded between 'one-star' and 'five-star'. There are also 'hotels without a star' and 'guesthouses'.

Generally Cyprus's newer hotels are very good, although the traditional design of older hotels may be to the liking of many travellers.

Modern hotels

These are spacious, well decorated and efficiently run. However, the plumbing can be erratic and some balcony rails may be too low for real safety. Hotels with two-star rating and below seem most vulnerable to maintenance difficulties.

Swimming-pool users should realise that underwater obstructions and unexpected shallow areas have caused injuries at some hotels.

Old hotels

The new towns do not have many older hotels, but most of the hill resorts have nothing else. Some are very good, but most are likely to be in need of maintenance. Some cheap one-star hotels are somewhat unsatisfactory.

Facilities

These are determined by the star rating given. A single-star is likely to be a small hotel or apartment block. It will offer air-conditioned twin rooms with en-suite bathroom, telephone, TV and room service, and will have a bar and restaurant, laundry, car park and lift depending on the number of storeys.

A two-star establishment will offer medium-sized accommodation with all of the above, but on a larger scale – a pool and terraces, possibly a shop and some evening entertainment.

Three-star and over is for larger hotels and complexes with a range of facilities, restaurants and evening entertainment. Some have spas, steam baths, saunas, solariums, beauty parlours and gymnasiums.

Availability

Accommodation currently exceeds demand and last-minute deals can be obtained. Nevertheless, the high season is a busy time.

Reception

English is spoken. Money and traveller's cheques can be changed, but the banks and shops give better rates. Telephone calls can be made from the room and are cheap in some hotels.

Meals

At hotels where meals may be included, these range from Cypriot cuisine to 'international', with theme nights such as a barbecue evening. Breakfasts are variable. A three-star hotel will provide a Cypriot, continental and English breakfast, all with fresh fruit. A two-star hotel may charge extra for the English breakfast.

Extras

Where air conditioning is not centrally provided, individual units can be used at a predetermined charge per day per unit.

Reservations

The **Cyprus Tourism Organisation (CTO)**'s office at Larnaka Airport can assist incoming passengers with hotel reservations (*tel: 24 008 368*) and so can the **Cyprus Tourism** office at Pafos Airport (*tel: 26 007 368*).
There is also assistance at **Lemesos port** (*tel: 25 571 868*).
In the north, the **Northern Cyprus Hoteliers Association** publishes an excellent annual hotel guide.
Tel: 815 8758. www.northcyprus.net

Rates

Rates are generally inclusive of breakfast, a 10 per cent service charge and tax.

Discounts vary remarkably from 10 to 50 per cent during April and October and during the low tourist season, which for seaside resorts is November, February and March. Children under 2 years stay free, 3–6 years at 50 per cent and 7–12 years at a 25 per cent reduction on rates.

In the following list of recommended hotels and apartments, the price rating indicates the approximate cost per room per night in high season and including breakfast. (Note that the Republic of Cyprus now uses the euro.)

£	Up to €80/YTL150
££	€80–150/YTL150–230
£££	Over €150/YTL230

LEFKOSIA
Centrum ££
Expect spacious, clean and comfortable rooms in an unbeatable location in the old town. Free Wi-Fi.
Pasikratous 15, Plateia Eleftherias.
Tel: 22 456 444. www.centrumhotel.net

SOUTHEAST
Agia Napa
Bella Napa ££
The hotel has extensive facilities and is situated about 1km (²/₃ mile) from the town centre and some 300m (330yds) from the nearest beach.
47 Leoforos Kryou Nerou. Tel: 23 819 900.
Napa Mermaid ££
All rooms overlook the sea. The hotel is about 100m (110yds) from the beach.
Leoforos Kryou Nerou 45. Tel: 23 721 606.
www.napamermaidhotel.com.cy

Larnaka

Louis Princess Beach £££
Excellent hotel on long
beach with choice of
restaurants and bars.
Oroklini,
Larnaka–Dhekelia road.
Tel: 24 645 500.
www.louishotels.com

Protaras

Grecian Park £££
Quality, comfort and
panoramic views over
Cape Gkreko. Regular
courtesy buses to Agia
Napa are available.
Konnos 18, between Agia
Napa and Protaras.
Tel: 23 844 000.
www.grecianpark.com

SOUTH
Lemesos

The Four Seasons £££
Best luxury hotel (no
relation to the Four
Seasons chain) with
outstanding level of
service and comfort.
Leoforos Amathous.
Tel: 25 858 000.
www.fourseasons.com.cy

Londa £££
The chic contemporary
décor is a breath of fresh
air and the lobby bar is
the place to be in
Lemesos.

Georgiou 72.
Tel: 25 865 555.
www.londahotel.com

Pissouri Bay
Columbia Beach
Resort £££
This gorgeous resort
oozes Mediterranean
style. Big swimming
pools, excellent spa and
superb restaurants, all
overlooking a lovely
beach.
Pissouri Bay.
Tel: 25 833 333.
www.columbia-hotels.com

WEST
Pafos

Paphian Bay ££
A good seafront
location by the
beach and about 3km
(2 miles) to the life of
Kato Pafos.
Leoforos Poseidonos,
Geroskipou.
Tel: 26 964 333.

Almyra £££
The chic, contemporary
Almyra manages to be
ideal for both couples
seeking romance and
parents seeking a
break from the kids –
their children's
programmes are
renowned.

Leoforos Poseidonos.
Tel: 26 888 700.
www.thanoshotels.com

Polis

Anassa £££
This elegant hotel has
lush gardens, an
excellent spa, and the
best location in Cyprus,
at the edge of the
Akamas Peninsula.
Neo Chorio, Latchi.
Tel: 26 888 000.
www.thanoshotels.com

TROODOS
Kakopetria

The Mill ££
This family-owned hotel
is delightfully set in a
renovated mill. Rooms
are spacious and
comfortable.
Milos 8. Tel: 22 922 536.
www.cymillhotel.com

NORTH
Beylerbeyi (Bellapaïs)

Bellapaïs Gardens ££
High above Girne, this
beautiful family-owned
property offers
personable service, a
superb restaurant,
and private two-storey
suites in gorgeous
gardens with jaw-
dropping views.

Crusader Rd.
Tel: 815 6066. www.
bellapaisgardens.com

Girne
Dome ££
This big old-fashioned
hotel has spacious rooms
with balconies, a
wonderful swimming pool
and fabulous sea views.
Kordonboyu.
Tel: 815 2453. www.
dome-cyprus.com
Nostalgia ££
A restored old house
with 28 rooms and pool.
Cafer Paşa 22, near
the harbour.
Tel: 815 3079.
nostalgia@northcyprus.net

Karpaz Yarımadası (Dipkarpaz)
Karpaz Arch Houses £
Rustic rooms in an
atmospheric old stone
building.
Dipkarpaz village,
northern Cyprus.
Tel: 372 2009. www.
karpazarchhouses.com

Lefkoşa
City Royal ££
Modern hotel with
casino and health centre.
Kemal Aşık 19.
Tel: 228 7621.

OTHER ACCOMMODATION
Campsites
Basic facilities usually
with mini-markets and
a simple taverna.

Lemesos
Governor's Beach
Tents can be hired.
20km (12½ miles) east of
Lemesos, junction 16 off
the Lefkosia–Lemesos
motorway.
Tel: 25 632 878.
Open: all year.

Pafos
Coral Bay (Feggari Camping Ltd)
A new site near the
beach.
13km (8 miles) north of
Pafos. Tel: 26 621 534.
Open: all year.
Geroskipou Zenon Gardens
Site on the beach.
East of Geroskipou Tourist
Beach, 3km (2 miles)
southeast of Pafos
harbour. Tel: 99 632 229.
Open: Apr–Oct.

Polis
A very popular site.
On the beach, 10 minutes
from town. Tel: 26 815 080.
Open: Mar–end Oct.

Troodos
A site 1,700m (5,577ft)
above sea level; spaces
are allocated among the
pine trees.
2km (1¼ miles) north of
Troodos Hill Resort, just
off the main
Lefkosia–Troodos Rd.
Tel: 25 420 205. Open:
May–Oct.

Village houses
Cyprus also caters for
visitors who care about
the countryside. In the
project, which aims to
put money directly into
the villages, the houses
maintain their original
exteriors but are
renovated within.

Youth hostels
These are to be found in
the larger towns of
Lefkosia, Lemesos,
Larnaka and Pafos.
They are open to non-
members with a 'guest
pass'. But there are also
rural hostels – one in
the hills near Mount
Olympos and another in
the Pafos forest.
Cyprus Youth Hostel
Association.
Tel: 22 670 027
(see p187).

Practical guide

Arriving

By air

The national carrier of the south is **Cyprus Airways** (*www.cyprusairways. com*) with flights to Larnaka and Pafos from London, Birmingham and Manchester. **Flythomascook** (*www. flythomascook.com*) flies to Pafos from Birmingham, Bristol, Cardiff, East Midlands, Glasgow, Luton, Manchester, Newcastle and Stansted, and into Larnaka. There are direct flights to Cyprus from Dubai with **Emirates** (*www.emirates.com*) and many of the Middle East's low-cost airlines. In the north, **Pegasus** (*www.flypgs.com*) connects northern Cyprus with many European cities while Turkish Airlines and Atlas Jet travel via Istanbul.

In the south of the island there are two new and spacious airports, Larnaka and Pafos (*tel: 24 816 400*). Larnaka in the east is 6km (3³/4 miles) from the town. Pafos Airport is smaller, 13km (8 miles) from the town.

Most nationals require only a passport; this broadly covers visitors from the European Union, the Commonwealth and the United States.

Generally, citizens of countries not in the EU receive a stamp in their passport that allows a stay of three months. No vaccination or health certificates are required for visitors.

There are buses to the airports operated by OSYRA (*www.pafosbuses. com*) and Intercity Buses (*www.intercity-buses.com*), and there are plenty of taxis (*see p187*). Those on package deals will be met by a representative of the company and taken to their resort.

Flights to north Cyprus arrive at Ercan Airport, 37km (23 miles) from Girne (Kyrenia) and 48km (30 miles) from Gazimağusa (Famagusta). No airline flies direct; all have to stop in Turkey to comply with formalities. If asked, the immigration officer will stamp a piece of paper rather than the passport. Stamps from the north in your passport may prevent future entry to southern Cyprus. The Greek-Cypriot government once declared all visitors arriving in the north as illegal immigrants, although this policy looks set to change under the new president.

By boat

Passenger services connect Cyprus with Piraeus, Rhodes (Greece), Haifa, Ashdod (Israel) and Port Said (Egypt). These sailings are from Lemesos. Regular services do not commence until the spring; winter services depend a great deal upon weather conditions.

In north Cyprus, a daily ferry connects Kyrenia with Taşucu, Selifke and Antalya in southern Turkey. From Gazimağusa (Famagusta) there is a year-round passenger- and car-ferry service to Mersin in Turkey. Here too, the immigration officer will forgo the passport stamp if asked.

Departure
Charter flights are always part of a package, and though confirmation is not necessary, they are notorious for being delayed. Try to check if the flight is late before leaving the hotel. Being called to the departure lounge is no guarantee that departure is imminent.

Camping
Camping is only permitted on approved sites licensed by the tourist office. There are various such sites in the south and north and the amenities provided generally include electricity, toilets and showers, café and washing facilities, though the standard varies from site to site. Fees are about €10–25 per day for a tent or caravan space plus tax. Many of the sites have tents available for hire (*see p173*).

Children
Children are generally safe, though care should be taken to prevent them getting sunburnt. The other main dangers are at archaeological sites where unguarded battlements and unprotected drops are common. Nappies and baby food are easily available.

Climate
Cyprus is the hottest and driest island in the Mediterranean. It starts getting hot in May, and by July and August it is more than 30°C (86°F) on the coast and often above 38°C (100°F) inland.

There is rarely any rain between June and September and very little in May and October. In the mountains it is much cooler at night, but even here during the day it is still relatively hot. The sea is warm from the end of May to October.

December to April is still mild, but the weather is changeable and evenings can be cool. It can get very cold and rainy in many parts of Cyprus. It also gets dark early. April is the height of the spring but by late summer the landscape becomes very dry and dusty.

Crime
While there may be the occasional bag-snatching incident, there is little crime in Cyprus. Any problem in this respect is unlikely to be with the

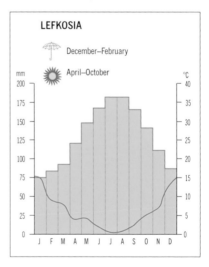

WEATHER CONVERSION CHART

25.4mm = 1 inch

°F = 1.8 × °C + 32

Practical guide

Cypriots, for they are generally honest and law-abiding. However, like anywhere else, reasonable care should be taken over property. For example, the car should be locked with belongings stored in the boot; money and jewellery ought to be kept in the hotel safe. In the event of any incident the police should be contacted and they are generally very helpful. Policemen usually speak English. Hotel prices should be displayed on the room door and taxi prices in the vehicle; this should avoid unpleasant misunderstandings.

Customs regulations

EU citizens may bring into the south for their personal use: 200 cigarettes or 100 cigarillos or 50 cigars or 250g tobacco; 4 litres wine; 1 litre spirits; 2 litres fortified wines such as sherry and port; and 16 litres beer.

It is prohibited to bring in bulbs, cut flowers, fruit, vegetables, seeds and cuttings, or any form of weaponry or drugs.

Visitors to the north may bring in duty free: 400 cigarettes or 500g tobacco or 1.5 litres spirits; 1.5 litres wine; and 100cl perfume.

While there is no restriction on the amount of currency imported or exported in the south, amounts over €10,000 or its equivalent in any currency must be declared. Currency, liquor and tobacco cannot be taken from the north to the south.

Driving

Accidents

If you have an accident, call *112* and wait until the police arrive. Take a photograph of the scene, and exchange numbers with any witnesses.

Breakdowns

Hire-car companies issue a phone number to call in case of breakdown. Those travelling in the south with their own cars may be able to use:

Cyprus Automobile Association
12 Chr. Mylonas, Lefkosia.
Tel: 22 313 233. www.caa.com.cy

Driving standards

The roads are reasonable in Cyprus (but Cypriots can be reckless drivers). However, you must take care at all times, particularly on mountain roads, and make sure that your screen wash is topped up, as roads get very dusty at the height of summer. Cars also get extremely hot if they are not parked in the shade and it is worth using a windscreen blind, or at least covering the steering wheel and leaving the windows slightly open. Seat belts must be worn in front and rear seats at all times. It is illegal to use a mobile phone while driving. There is random breath-testing. Limit: 22mg of alcohol (39mg in the north) in 100ml of breath.

Finding your way

Finding your way is generally easy. Signposts are in English and Greek and the main tourist sites are marked with distinctive brown signs. Village streets have maze-like qualities and no signs, but follow your instincts and chances are you will emerge at the other side of the village. With a large car, it may be unwise even to attempt the narrower streets.

Motorists should beware of instructions given by locals. Directions drawn out with a stick in the dust should be treated with even more circumspection. Drivers should also beware of the statement 'the road is good'.

Visitors should be aware that some of the spellings of place names have been changed. For example, Larnaca has become Larnaka and Khirokitia changes to Choirokoitia.

Car hire
There is an inordinate number of car-hire companies in Cyprus, from the big international names to tiny local firms. The minimum age limit required by most firms is 21 and a national driving licence is required. Drivers under 25 who have held a full licence for less than three years need to inform the rental company, so that insurance can be arranged. There are four types of cars, type A being the smallest and cheapest. Open-top jeeps seem to be popular vehicles.

Check what the price of hire includes, particularly for collision damage waiver, without which visitors are responsible for any damage caused. Also scrutinise the state of the car, paying special attention to tyres and brakes.

Hiring a car is a great way of exploring the island

Very competitive rates are available to visitors who seek out the best prices and book in advance and online. It is much easier than hunting around in Cyprus.

In the north, car hire is cheaper but the same principles apply. Most confusing is the fact that some firms hire out both left- and right-hand drive cars, despite the fact that driving in the north and in the south is on the left.

Parking

Parking is generally, but not always, easy. There are car parks in all the major towns. No parking is allowed on double yellow lines and only loading and unloading on single yellow lines.

Petrol

There are a large number of petrol stations across the island, but most are shut on Sundays and bank holidays. However, many petrol stations have petrol vending machines. Manned stations close at 6 or 7pm on weekdays and at 3pm on Saturdays. Some close at 2pm on Tuesday or Wednesday.

Speed limits

The speed limit on all main highways is 100km/h (62mph), with a lower limit of 65km/h (40mph). Other rural roads: 80km/h (50mph). In towns: 50km/h (31mph). Distances in the south are in kilometres and in the north in miles.

Electricity

The electricity supply is 240 volts AC 50 cycles single-phase for lighting and domestic requirements. Socket outlets are for three-pin plugs. Hotels generally have a 110-volt outlet for shavers.

Embassies and consulates

South

Australian High Commission
Annis Komninis 4, 2nd Floor, 1060 Lefkosia. Tel: 22 753 001.

British High Commission
Alexander Pallis, PO Box 21978, 1106 Lefkosia. Tel: 22 861 100.

US Embassy
Gonia Metochiou and Ploutarchou, Lefkosia. Tel: 22 393 939.

North

Australian High Commission
20 Güner Türkmen Sokağı, Lefkoşa. Tel: 227 7332.

British High Commission Consular Section
Mehmet Akif Caddesi, Lefkoşa. Tel: 227 4938.

US Embassy, American Centre
20 Güner Türkmen Sokağı, Lefkoşa. Tel: 227 2443.

Emergency telephone numbers

South

Emergency operators speak English.

Ambulance *112*
Fire Service *112*
Police *112*
Forest fire *1407*
Night pharmacies *192*

General hospitals
Lefkosia *22 603 000*
Lemesos *25 801 100*
Larnaka *24 800 500*
Pafos *26 821 800*
Paralimni *23 821 211*
Polis *26 321 431*

North
Police *155*
First aid *112*
Fire *199*
Forest fire *177*
Hospitals
Lefkoşa *228 5441*
Girne *815 2266*

Entry to the north from the south

For visitors arriving in the south the journey across the 'Green Line' should officially be on a return journey. There are seven points of access along the 137km (85-mile) division, the best known being at the old Ledra Palace Hotel in Lefkosia. The others are at Ledra Street, Metehan and Agios Dometios, also in Lefkosia, Strovilia and Pergamos in the east and the new Limnitis crossing near Kato Pyrgos. Passports are required. Clearance has to be obtained from the police at the Greek checkpoint, who will record your passport number. Then walk through to the Turkish side. Here you will have to fill out a form. Since the border was opened to Greek and Turkish Cypriots in 2003, things have been more relaxed.

People wishing to go further afield than Lefkosia can hire a taxi or a car.

Hired cars are rarely allowed through the control point. You can get taxis on both sides of the border.

Alternatively, opt for a bus. Most buses leave from Girne Gate.

Etiquette

In monasteries, remember that shoulders and legs need to be covered. In mosques, women also need to wear a headscarf and long skirt. Shorts, backless dresses or tops that leave the shoulders exposed may cause offence.

Health

There are no inoculation requirements and no health certificates needed. Medical facilities must be paid for and visitors are strongly advised to take out holiday insurance.

EU citizens should bring a European Health Insurance Card (EHIC), which entitles the bearer to free basic healthcare. This card is available free online (*www.ehic.org.uk*), by phone (*0845 606 2030*), or from post offices.

General hospitals have casualty departments for emergency cases. Hotels will make arrangements for medical services for their guests upon request. Private doctors' surgeries are usually open weekdays, 9am–1pm and 4–7pm.

Cyprus has a healthy climate and the water is safe to drink. However, wash all fruit and salad vegetables. Sunburn can be a problem. Even one hour in the sun on the first day will be enough to cause the fair-skinned to burn.

Mosquitoes, although not malarial, are sometimes a nuisance. If the room is air-conditioned, kill them before going to bed and keep the windows closed. Where windows have to be open, a mosquito coil may help. Insect repellent should also be used.

There are at least two types of venomous snakes in Cyprus. One is the viper, identified by its distinctive zigzag markings. It is unlikely to be encountered, but walkers and climbers in the hills, especially the Beşparmak Mountains, need to keep a watch out. If bitten, keep movement to a minimum and seek medical attention immediately. A serum is available on order from pharmacies for those who feel confident enough to use it.

Hitchhiking

Hitchhiking is allowed, although single women are not encouraged to do so, especially in outlying areas at night. Visitors are most likely to be approached for lifts by young soldiers on leave from military service trying to return home.

Insurance

Some form of holiday insurance is recommended. The important priority is to ensure that it covers medical expenses.

Driving insurance is included in the price of car hire. Check that it includes a collision damage waiver.

Car insurance will not cover the underside of the car, so care is needed on bad roads. Citizens of non-EU countries with their own cars will need a green card.

Lost property

The Cypriots are honest people and lost items are often quickly returned to their owners. Failing that, the local police station should be contacted. The loss of insured items and traveller's cheques should also be immediately reported to the responsible authority listed in the documentation.

Maps

There are free road and town maps available from the Cyprus Tourism Organisation. The North Cyprus Tourist Office also issues a useful free road map with town plans. The best large-scale maps are the British Ministry of Defence series K. Difficult to get, but try the **Department of Lands and Surveys**, Lefkosia (*tel: 22 402 890*).

Measurements

Cyprus uses metric weights and measures. Clothes and shoes use standard European sizes (*see p185*).

Media

Greek Cyprus has many daily and weekly newspapers. The daily *Cyprus Mail* (*www.cyprus-mail.com*) is in English, as is the *Cyprus Weekly*. English and other European newspapers are on sale, usually one day late. In the Turkish part of Cyprus the *Cyprus Times* is in English but publication has now become infrequent.

Three government-controlled radio channels are transmitted in the south. There are many private stations of which Rock FM puts out most programmes in English. BFBS is the British Forces Broadcasting Service and it is on the air on two channels for 24 hours. Northern Cyprus can also tune into all these stations.

Television programmes by Cyprus Broadcasting (CYBC) in the government-controlled area are transmitted on two channels throughout the day. Other channels include Greek Television.

In the north, local television is by BRT. Viewers can tune into Turkish television and get news in English. Satellite television is widely available all over Cyprus.

Money matters
Banks

Language is not usually a serious problem as most bank clerks do speak good English.

Banks are open Monday to Friday 8.30am–12.30pm, as well as Monday 3.15–4.45pm. However, in all the tourist areas many banks offer afternoon services. They are open to exchange money from 3 to 5pm, sometimes to 7pm. At the airport, banks are open all day and also offer night services.

Many hotels have exchange facilities though they do charge a higher commission than the banks.

Banks in north Cyprus are open 8am–noon (summer) and 8am–noon & 2–4pm (winter). Shops, restaurants and hotels accept major credit cards.

Money can also be withdrawn from the principal banks and there are an increasing number of automatic cash dispensers which take credit cards. Thomas Cook traveller's cheques in sterling are accepted by most hotels although traveller's cheques are accepted less now than they were in the past.

North

The north does not have a currency. In use is the New Turkish lira (YTL), introduced in 2005. YTL1 = one million old lira. Old lira notes are not legal tender. YTL1 = 100 kurus. Notes are in denominations of YTL1, 5, 10, 20, 50 and 100. Coins cover values of 5, 10, 20, 50 and 100 kurus. Euros, pounds and US dollars are widely accepted.

South

Greek-Cypriot currency is the euro, which is divided into 100 cents. There are notes to the value of €5, €10, €20, €50, €100 and €500 and coins in denominations of 1, 2, 5, 10, 20 and 50 cents, and 1 and 2 euros (*see also* Customs regulations, *p176*).

Language

Cyprus has always had two official languages, Modern Greek and Turkish. The present division of the island means that Greek is spoken in the south and Turkish in the north. There is no absolute need for English-speakers to learn Greek, for almost all Greek Cypriots, including all those in the tourist industry, speak good English. French and Italian are also spoken in tourist areas. However, an attempt at the language is always well received in the village coffee shop and similar places, and will probably lead to further conversation.

GREEK
Useful words and phrases

yes	né
no	óhi
please	parakaló
thank you	efcharistó
hello	yásou
goodbye	chérete
good morning	kaliméra
good afternoon	kalispéra
goodnight	kaliníkta
today	símera
tomorrow	ávrio
yesterday	hthes
Sunday	kiriakí
Monday	theftéra
Tuesday	tríti
Wednesday	tetárti
Thursday	pémpti
Friday	paraskeví
Saturday	sávaton
bank	trápeza
bus	leoforío
car	aftokínito

Where is ...?	pou iné ...?
How much?	póso káni?
Do you speak English?	milate angliká?
a room	domátio

Numbers

1	éna
2	dío
3	tría
4	téssera
5	pénte
6	éxi
7	eptá
8	októ
9	ennía
10	déka
20	íkosi
100	ekató
200	diakosia
500	pentakósia
1,000	chília

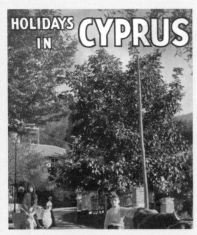

An old holiday poster

North

In the north, English is also spoken. Waiters will have a limited fluency, and some knowledge of Turkish is a definite advantage.

Signs have Turkish names for places, as do maps, so it is wise if coming from the south to have a map showing Turkish names.

Greek	Turkish
Kyrenia	Girne
Ammochostos	Gazimağusa
Morfou	Güzelyurt
Lefkosia	Lefkoşa
Lapithos	Lapta
Pentadaktylos	Beşparmak

The Turkish alphabet is very similar to the Latin script with a few exceptions:
c = j as in jam   u = u as in French tu
ç = ch   ı = a as in serial
s = sh

TURKISH
Useful words and phrases

yes	evet
no	hayir
please	lutfen
thank you	mersi
hello	merhaba
goodbye	allahaismarladik
good morning	gunyadin
good evening	iyi aksamlar
goodnight	iyi geceler
today	bugun
tomorrow	yarin
yesterday	dun
sorry	özür dilerim
How much?	ne kadar?
Sunday	Pazar
Monday	Pazartesi
Tuesday	Sali
Wednesday	Carsamba
Thursday	Persembe
Friday	Cuma
Saturday	Cumartesi

Numbers

1	bir	30	otuz
2	iki	40	kirk
3	uc	50	elli
4	dort	60	altmis
5	bes	70	yetmis
6	alti	80	seksen
7	yedi	90	doksan
8	sekiz	100	yuz
9	dokuz	200	iki yuz
10	on	300	uc yuz
11	on bir	1,000	bin
20	yirmi	2,000	iki bin

National holidays

All public services, private enterprises and shops are officially closed on national holidays. In resort and coastal areas, however, shops and certain services remain open.

Southern Cyprus
1 January New Year's Day
6 January Epiphany Day
Variable Green Monday (50 days before Greek Orthodox Easter)
25 March Greek Independence Day
1 April Greek-Cypriot National Day
Variable Good Friday (Greek Orthodox Church)
Variable Easter Sunday
Variable Easter Monday (Greek Orthodox Church)
1 May Labour Day
Variable Kataklysmos (Festival of the Flood – Pentecost)
15 August Dormition of the Virgin Mary (Assumption)
1 October Cyprus Independence Day
28 October Greek National Day (Okhi Day)
24–26 December Christmas

Northern Cyprus
1 January New Year's Day
23 April Children's Festival (also known as National Sovereignty Day)
1 May Labour Day
19 May Youth and Sports Day
20 July Peace and Freedom Day (anniversary of the Ottoman conquest of Famagusta in 1571)

1 August Social Resistance Day (in remembrance of Turkish-Cypriot struggle for partition)
30 August Victory Day
29 October Turkish Republic Day (anniversary of declaration of Independent Republic of Turkey, 1923)
15 November Republic Day (anniversary of 1983 ratification of Constitution by Turkish Cypriots)
The main Muslim holidays, Bayram at the end of the Ramadan Seker and the four-day Kurban Bayram (Feast of the Sacrifice), move through the calendar.

Opening times
Southern Cyprus
Shops and businesses
Summer (1 May–30 Sept): Mon–Tue & Thur–Fri 7am–1pm & 5–8pm, Wed 8am–3pm, Sat 8am–7.30pm.
Winter (1 Oct–30 Apr): Mon–Tue & Thur–Fri 8am–1pm & 2.30–7.30pm, Wed 8am–3pm, Sat 8am–7pm.

Some shops do not close for lunch, while others close on Saturday afternoons. In the tourist areas, supermarkets and souvenir shops open until late in the evening and all day Sunday.

Public services
Summer (1 Jul–31 Aug): Mon–Fri 7.30am–2pm.
Winter (1 Sept–30 Jun): Mon–Wed & Fri 7.30am–2.30pm, Thur 7.30am–2.30pm & 3–6pm.

Northern Cyprus
Shops
Summer: 8am–1pm & 4–7pm.
Winter: 9am–1pm & 2–6pm.
Early closing Saturday and closed all day Sunday. Opening all day is becoming fairly common.

Business hours
Summer: 8am–noon.
Winter: Mon–Fri 8am–noon & 2–4pm.

Public services
Summer: Mon 7.30am–2pm & 3.30–6pm, Tue–Fri 7.30am–2pm.
Winter: 8am–1pm & 2–5pm.

Organised tours
Those on package deals will have plenty of tours organised for them. These will usually be by bus; but although they are a good way of getting away from the resorts, they may be too inflexible for the independently minded.

Boat trips from Pafos to Lara; from Latchi to the Akamas Peninsula; and from Agia Napa to Cape Gkreko. Hiking and jeep excursions to the hinterland are also available.

For specific details, contact hotel reception or the tourist office, who have a list of approved tour operators.

Photography
In the south and north there are many photography shops selling memory cards and film and offering good-quality transfer and developing services.

CONVERSION TABLE

FROM	TO	MULTIPLY BY
Inches	Centimetres	2.54
Feet	Metres	0.3048
Yards	Metres	0.9144
Miles	Kilometres	1.6090
Acres	Hectares	0.4047
Gallons	Litres	4.5460
Ounces	Grams	28.35
Pounds	Grams	453.6
Pounds	Kilograms	0.4536
Tons	Tonnes	1.0160

To convert back, for example from centimetres to inches, divide by the number in the third column.

MEN'S SUITS

UK	36	38	40	42	44	46	48
Cyprus & Rest of Europe	46	48	50	52	54	56	58
USA	36	38	40	42	44	46	48

DRESS SIZES

UK	8	10	12	14	16	18
France	36	38	40	42	44	46
Italy	38	40	42	44	46	48
Cyprus & Rest of Europe	34	36	38	40	42	44
USA	6	8	10	12	14	16

MEN'S SHIRTS

UK	14	14.5	15	15.5	16	16.5	17
Cyprus & Rest of Europe	36	37	38	39/40	41	42	43
USA	14	14.5	15	15.5	16	16.5	17

MEN'S SHOES

UK	7	7.5	8.5	9.5	10.5	11
Cyprus & Rest of Europe	41	42	43	44	45	46
USA	8	8.5	9.5	10.5	11.5	12

WOMEN'S SHOES

UK	4.5	5	5.5	6	6.5	7
Cyprus & Rest of Europe	38	38	39	39	40	41
USA	6	6.5	7	7.5	8	8.5

There are restricted areas near military camps and the Green Line, where photography is forbidden. Flash is not permitted inside churches, and museums require a permit.

Places of worship

The religion of southern Cyprus is Greek Orthodox. There are services every Saturday evening and Sunday morning. Mosques are more common in the north.

Anglican churches

Larnaka St Helena's, *St Helena Building, Flat 20l.*
Lefkosia St Paul's, *Leoforos Vyronos.*
Lemesos St Barnabas, *Archiepiskopou Leontiou 153.*
Pafos Chrysopolitissa Church, *Kato Pafos.*
Anglican services (other denominations welcome) are held every Sunday at St Andrew's Church, near Girne Castle.

Roman Catholic churches

Larnaka Santa Maria Church, *Terra Santa St.*
Lefkosia Roman Catholic Church (Holy Cross), *Pyli Pafou.*
Lemesos St Catherine's, *Jerousalim 2.*
Pafos Chrysopolitissa Church, *Kato Pafos.*

Mosques

Omeriye Mosque, *Trikoupi, Lefkosia.* Prayer every Friday afternoon.

There are mosques in all towns in northern Cyprus.

Police

Cypriot police are usually helpful and most speak English. There are also tourist office assistants in the resorts who will help visitors in trouble. The general emergency number is *112*.

Post offices
South

Main post offices are:
Larnaka *Plateia Vasileos Pavlou. Tel: 24 802 406.*
Lefkosia *Plateia Eleftherias. Tel: 22 303 219.*
Lemesos *Gladstonos 3. Tel: 25 802 259.*
Pafos *Nikodimou Mylona. Tel: 26 818 520.*
Open: Jul–Aug Mon–Fri 7.30am–1pm & 3–5.30pm, Sat 9–11am; Sept–Jun Mon–Tue & Thur–Fri 7.30am–1.30pm & 3–6pm, Wed 7.30am–1.30pm, Sat 9–11am.

Other post offices close Saturday and afternoons year-round except from September to June on Thursdays.

Airmail letters take three to four days to reach the rest of Europe.

North

All post from northern Cyprus goes via Turkey. Post offices in the north open: Mon–Fri 8am–noon & 2–4pm, Sat 8am–noon.

Public transport
South
Buses

Inter-city and village buses operate between the main towns. Village buses tend to serve local needs, coming into town early in the morning and returning early afternoon.

There are regular services between the main towns until about 7pm. There are also frequent services between out-of-town hotels and the town centres or the beach. Information should be available at the hotels.

Main bus stations
Lefkosia *Plateia Solomou, west of Plateia Eleftherias on the walls. Tel: 22 665 814, 22 778 841.*
Larnaka *King Evagora 2. Tel: 24 650 477.*
Lemesos *A. Themistocleous 7. Tel: 25 370 592.*
Pafos *Karavella bus station, Mesoqi. Tel: 26 934 410.*

Taxis
Service taxis (shared taxis) operate between the main towns, usually every half-hour. There are no service taxis to the airport or on Sundays. Seats can be booked in advance. Urban taxis are available in the main towns and serving the airports. Fares are higher after midnight and there is usually an extra charge for luggage.
No service taxis on public holidays.

North
Taxis offer both individual services and shared taxi routes. There are buses connecting Lefkoşa with

Girne and Güzelyurt (Morfou) three times an hour. There is an hourly bus from Girne to Gazimağusa. The timetable is somewhat flexible and the last buses can be around 6pm.

There is a good network connecting many of the villages. Fares are cheap.

Senior citizens
Few concessions are made for the elderly or those with disabilities. Most of the villages and many parts of the towns lack a complete pavement. Most hotels have ramps.

Student and youth travel
Cyprus is not on the backpacker's route. Budget accommodation is fairly limited.

The Youth Card Euro<26 is a European service for young people aged 13–26 and entitles them to discounts on products and services in Cyprus. There are some campsites (*see p173*) and the following is a popular youth hostel:
Troodos *400m (440yds) from Troodos Sq on Kakopetria–Troodos Rd. Tel: 25 420 200. Open: Apr–Oct daily 7.30–10.30am & 4–10pm.*
For further information contact:
Cyprus Youth Hostel Association
PO Box 24040, Lefkosia. Tel: 22 670 027.

Sustainable tourism
Thomas Cook is a strong advocate of ethical and fairly traded tourism and

believes that the travel experience should be as good for the places visited as it is for the people who visit them. That's why we firmly support The Travel Foundation, a charity that develops solutions to help improve and protect holiday destinations, their environment, traditions and culture. To find out what you can do to make a positive difference to the places you travel to and the people who live there, please visit *www.makeholidaysgreener.org.uk*

Telephones
Cyprus has direct dialling to most countries from call boxes (CYTA, *www.cytanet.com.cy*). However, all towns have ones that take only emergency *112* calls. Telephone enquiries: dial *11892*. Instructions in the south are displayed in Greek and English. There is an increasing number of card phones taking cards to the value of €5, €10 and €20 (available from kiosks, post offices and banks). In the north, *cetones* (tokens) are used instead of coins. They come in three denominations and are obtained from kiosks and shops.

For international calls to south Cyprus dial *00357;* for north Cyprus *00 90 392*, followed by the number.

International codes
United Kingdom *00 44*
USA and **Canada** *00 1*
Australia *00 61*
Netherlands *00 31*

Local codes
South:
No codes, one complete number.
North:
Lefkoşa (Lefkosia) *227, 228*
Gazimağusa (Famagusta) *366*
Girne (Kyrenia) *815*
Güzelyurt (Morfou) *714*
Lefke (Lefka) *728*

Time
Cyprus is two hours ahead of Greenwich Mean Time. For summer, clocks go forward one hour from the last Sunday in March to the last Sunday in October.

Tipping
A 10 per cent service charge is included in hotel and restaurant bills. Porters and hairdressers appreciate a small tip, as do taxi drivers in the south. In the north it is not usual to tip taxi drivers, but customs are changing.

Toilets
There are public toilets virtually everywhere in the south but very few in the north. Some are cleaner than others, but none has toilet paper. Paper should not be put down the toilet but left in the bin.

Tourist offices
South
Main office (postal enquiries only): *Leoforos Lemesou 19, PO Box 24535, 1390 Lefkosia. Tel: 22 691 100.*

Agia Napa
12 Leoforos Kyrou Nerou.
Tel: 23 721 796.
Larnaka
Plateia Vasileos Pavlou.
Tel: 24 654 322.
International Airport.
Tel: 24 643 576 (24 hours).
Lefkosia
Laiki Geitonia.
Tel: 22 674 264.
Lemesos
Lemesos harbour.
Tel: 25 571 868.
Potamos Tis Germasogeias,
Georgiou 22.
Tel: 25 323 211.
Spyros Araouzou 115.
Tel: 25 362 756.
Pafos
Gladstonos 3.
Tel: 26 932 841.
Leoforos Poseidonos 63A.
Tel: 26 930 521.
Pafos International Airport.
Tel: 26 007 368, service to
all flights.
Platres
Olymbou 4.
Tel: 25 421 316.
Tourist offices in many towns and
resorts are open Monday to Saturday.
They are closed Wednesday and
Saturday afternoons and Sunday.

North
Lefkoşa (Lefkosia)
Girne Gate, İnönü Sq.
Tel: 227 2994.

Gazimağusa (Famagusta)
5 Fevzi Çakmak Caddesi.
Tel: 366 2864.
Girne (Kyrenia)
Harbour.
Tel: 815 2145.

Airport tourist offices are open
24 hours a day between Monday
and Saturday.

Offices abroad
UK Cyprus Tourist Office
17 Hanover St, London W1S 1YP.
Tel: (020) 7569 8800.
UK North Cyprus Tourist Office
29 Bedford Sq, London WC1B 3EG.
Tel: (020) 7631 1930.
US Cyprus Tourist Organisation
13 East 40th St, New York 10016.
Tel: (212) 683 5280.

Travellers with disabilities
Cyprus has yet to provide much
in the way of facilities for travellers
with disabilities, although things are
improving. The tourist office
publishes a leaflet which gives useful
and detailed information. Travel agents
should also be able to give general
advice, and provide information on
suitable hotels.

Most villages and towns do not
have complete pavements, and there
are few ramps, Lefkosia being an
exception. The main resorts are on
fairly level ground, with the exception
of Agia Napa and the upper town
in Pafos.

Index

Acknowledgements

Thomas Cook Publishing wishes to thank the photographers, picture libraries and other organisations, to whom the copyright belongs, for the loan of the photographs in this book.

ACTION PUBLICATIONS 31, 56, 63, 90, 111, 113
STUART COXLEY 125
CYPRUS TOURISM 61, 107, 140, 146, 165
DREAMSTIME 65 (Robert Lerich), 93 (Bensliman), 110 (Yiannos1), 127 (Bruce Robbins), 150 (Ruzanna), 177 (Ferdericb)
I FERGUSSON-SHARP 41
CAROLE FRENCH 1, 12, 19, 22, 29, 35, 39, 81, 87
NORTHERN CYPRUS TOURIST BOARD 25, 121
PRESS AND INFORMATION OFFICE OF THE REPUBLIC OF CYPRUS 123 (John Samson)
SPECTRUM COLOUR LIBRARY 124, 132
THE THOMAS COOK ARCHIVE 7, 59, 80, 97, 137, 138, 145, 153, 155, 163, 183
WORLD PICTURES/PHOTOSHOT 14, 83, 122
The remaining pictures are held in the AA PHOTO LIBRARY and were taken by Malcolm Birkitt, with the exception of pages 115, 119, 130, 135, which were taken by Robert Bulmer, and pages 17, 54, 57, 70, which were taken by Roy Rainford.

For CAMBRIDGE PUBLISHING MANAGEMENT LIMITED:
Project editor: Ed Robinson
Typesetter: Paul Queripel
Proofreaders: Karolin Thomas & Jan McCann
Indexer: Marie Lorimer

SEND YOUR THOUGHTS TO
BOOKS@THOMASCOOK.COM

We're committed to providing the very best up-to-date information in our travel guides and constantly strive to make them as useful as they can be. You can help us to improve future editions by letting us have your feedback. If you've made a wonderful discovery on your travels that we don't already feature, if you'd like to inform us about recent changes to anything that we do include, or if you simply want to let us know your thoughts about this guidebook and how we can make it even better – we'd love to hear from you.

Send us ideas, discoveries and recommendations today and then look out for your valuable input in the next edition of this title.

Emails to the above address, or letters to the traveller guides Series Editor, Thomas Cook Publishing, PO Box 227, Coningsby Road, Peterborough PE3 8SB, UK.

Please don't forget to let us know which title your feedback refers to!